Edward Sylvester Ellis

The Ranger

The Fugitives of the Border

Edward Sylvester Ellis

The Ranger
The Fugitives of the Border

ISBN/EAN: 9783337350772

Printed in Europe, USA, Canada, Australia, Japan

Cover: Foto ©ninafisch / pixelio.de

More available books at **www.hansebooks.com**

THE RANGER;

OR,

THE FUGITIVES OF THE BORDER.

By EDWARD S. ELLIS,

AUTHOR OF "OONOMOO," "SETH JONES," "IRONA," ETC.

LONDON:

GEORGE ROUTLEDGE AND SONS,

THE BROADWAY, LUDGATE.

KENT, THE RANGER.

CHAPTER I.

ZEB AND HIS MASTER.

At the southern part of Ohio, where the river of that name swerves from its south-western course, and makes a sweeping bend toward the north-west, many years ago stood a large and imposing dwelling. Its character, so different and superior to others found here and there along the Ohio, showed that its owner must have been a man both of superior taste and abundant means. It had been built by Sir William Leland, who had emigrated from Europe with his young wife, and erected a home in the western wilderness. Here they lived a goodly number of days; and when, at last, they took their departure within a year of each other, they left behind them a son and daughter to cherish and inherit their home.

George Leland, at the time of which we speak, was but twenty, while his sister Rosalind was three years his junior. Yet both, with the assistance of a faithful negro servant, managed to live quite comfortably. The soil was exceedingly rich, and, with a little pains, yielded abundantly every thing that could be wished, while the river and wood were unfailing resources. Three years had elapsed since the elder Leland's death, and during that time, although living in a country swarming with Indians, nothing had occurred to alarm the fears of our friends, or even to give them the slightest suspicion that danger threatened them.

When Sir William settled in this section, he followed the example of the great founder of Pennsylvania, and purchased every foot of his land from those who claimed it; and, in addition to the liberal remuneration which each received, they were given some charming present by their pale-faced brother. This secured their friendship; and, although many miles intervened between the whites and their nearest kindred, yet they had nothing to fear from the savages who surrounded them. .Thus matters stood when George and Rosalind were left orphans, some years before the opening of our story.

It was a pleasant day in early summer that George and his sister were seated in front of their house. The sun was just setting, and they had remained thus a long time. Zeb, the negro, was absent for the time, and they were thus undisturbed.

"Do you really think," pursued the sister, "it can be true that the Indians have perpetrated the outrages which have been reported?"

"I should be glad to think differently, could I have reason for doing so; but these reports certainly have foundation; and what is more alarming, the suspicion that we are *not* safe, which was awakened some time ago, is now confirmed. For two or three days I have detected suspicious appearances, and Zeb informed me that he discovered a couple of savages lurking around the edge of the forest. I fear there is strong reason to apprehend danger."

"But, brother, will not the kindness which our parents showed them while living be a guaranty of our protection?"

"It may, to some extent; but you must remember that there are hundreds of Indians who have never seen or heard of them, who would not hesitate to kill or take us prisoners at the first opportunity."

"Can it be possible?"

"It is not only possible but true. You remember Roland Leslie, who was here last summer? Yesterday I saw him up the river, and he gave me the information that I have repeated. At first I deferred mentioning it to you, for the reason that I did not wish to alarm you until it could not be avoided."

"Why did he not come here?" asked the sister.

"He said that he should shortly visit us. He had heard rumors of another massacre some miles up the river, and wished to satisfy himself in regard to it before calling here. Leslie, although young, is an experienced hunter and backwoodsman, and I have not much fear for his personal safety. He assured me that, should he find the Indians above ravaging the country as fearfully as reported, he would immediately return to us."

"I hope so," earnestly replied Rosalind.

"Still," continued George, "what can we do, even then? He intends to bring a hunter back with him, and that will make only three of us against perhaps a thousand savages."

"But have we not the house to protect us?"

"And have they not the forest? Can they not lurk around until we die of hunger, or until they fire the building? There are a hundred contingencies that will bar an escape, while I confess no prospect of getting safely away presents itself."

"We have arms and ammunition," said Rosalind. "Of course Leslie and his friend are good marksmen, and why can we not do enough to deter and intimidate the savages? Finding us well prepared, they will doubtless retreat and not disturb us again. I hope the trouble will soon be over."

"I *hope* so too; but it is hoping against hope. This war will be a long and bloody one, and when it is over the country will present a different appearance. Many lives must be lost ere it is done, and perhaps ours are among that number."

"Perhaps so, brother; but do not be so depressed. Let us hope and pray for the best. It is not such a sad thing to die, and the country which has given us birth has certainly a strong claim upon us."

"Noble girl," exclaimed George, "it is so, and we have no cause for murmuring."

At this moment Zeb appeared. He was a short, dumpy, thick-set negro, with a most luxuriant head of wool, a portion of which hung around his head in small, close braids, resembling bits of decayed rope. His eyes were large and protruding, and his face glistened like a mirror. He was a genuine African. Some of their qualities in him were carried to the extreme. Instead of being a coward, as is often the case with his nation, he seemed never to know when there really was danger. He always was reckless and careless, and seemed to escape by accident.

"Heigh! massa George, what's up?" he exclaimed, observing the solemn appearance of the two before him.

"Nothing but what is known to you, Zeb. We were just speaking of the danger which you are aware is threatening us. Have you seen any thing lately to excite suspicion?"

" Nothin' worth speakin' of," replied he, seating himself in front of George and Rosalind.

" What was it, Zeb?" asked the latter.

" When I's out tendin' to things, I t'ought as how I'd sit down and rest, and 'cordin'ly I squats on a big stone. Purty soon de stone begin to move, and come to look, 'twas a big Injin.

" ' Heigh !' says I, ' what you doin' here?'

" ' Ugh !' he grunted.

" ' Yes, I'll ' ugh !' you,' says I, ' if I cotches you here ag'in.' With dat I pitches him two, free rods off, and tells him to make tracks fur home."

" Heavens ! if you would only tell the truth, Zeb. Did you really see an Indian, though?"

" 'Deed I did, and he run when he see'd me in arnist."

" And you saw others yesterday, did you ?" remarked Rosalind.

" Two or free, down toward de woods. I spied 'em crawlin' and smellin' down dar, and axes dem dar business. Dey said as how dey's lookin' for a jack-knife dat dey lost dar last summer. I told 'em dat dey oughter be 'shamed demselves to be smellin' round dat way ; and to provide against dar doin's iu future, I give dem each a good kick and sent dem away."

" Do not exaggerate your story so much," said Rosalind. " Give the truth and nothing else."

" Qua'r, folks won't believe all dis pusson observes," said he, with an offended air.

" Tell the truth and they will in all cases ; but should you deceive once, you will always be suspected afterward."

" Dat's it," commenced the negro, spreading out his broad hand like an orator to illustrate the point. " If I tells de truf dey're sure to t'ink I's lyin', and what's de use ?"

" Zeb," commenced George, not regarding the last remark, " you, as well as we, are aware that we are encompassed by peril. You have seen that the Indians are constantly prowling around, and evidently for no good purpose. What would you advise us to do under the circumstances ?"

" Give 'em all a good floggin' and set 'em to work," he replied.

"Come, come, Zeb, we want no jesting," interrupted Rosalind.

"Dar 'tis agin. Who war jestin'? Dat's what I t'ink is de best. Give 'em a good lickin', and set 'em to work clearin' off de wood till dar spunk is gone."

"Fudge!" said George, impatiently, turning his back toward Zeb, whose head ducked down with a chuckle.

"Rosalind," said George, "the best plan is certainly to wait until Leslie returns, which will be either to-morrow or the next day. We will then determine upon what course to pursue. Perhaps we shall be undisturbed until that time. If not, it can not be helped."

"Wished dis pusson warn't so hungry," remarked Zeb, picking up a stick and whittling it.

Rosalind smiled as she arose and remarked:

"It is getting late, George, and it perhaps is best to have supper."

He made no answer and turned toward the negro.

"Zeb," said he, "in all probability we shall be obliged to leave this place in a few days for a safer location. Of course you will accompany us, and I wish it to be understood that you are to lay aside this levity and carelessness. Remember that you are in danger, as much as ourselves. Your scalp may be the first taken."

"What, dis yere wool of mine? Yah! yah! yah! Lord bless you, dey'd have a handful!"

"How would you relish being roasted at the stake?" asked George, hoping to terrify him.

"Yah! yah! Dey'd be some sizzlin', I guess."

"You will think soberly about the matter, perhaps sooner than you suspect."

"Yas," said Zeb, and his face straightened out in an instant, while he slowly and thoughtfully continued whittling.

"Zeb," continued George, leaning toward him and speaking in an undertone, "I think we shall be attacked in two days at the latest."

"Jest keep de whip in good order, and I'll put it into 'em and teach 'em manners."

"I fear you will learn wisdom only by experience, even if you do then," returned George. "It would be a good thing

for you, should you meet with something that would impress
you with a sense of your peril.   I can only wonder at your
stupidity."

"Gorra mighty! do you s'pose dere's anything that'd make
me afeard of dem Injins?   Why, bless you, forty of 'em
wouldn't dare to frow a stone at me.   I've licked free, four
dozen of 'em, and dey all respect me awful."

"I suppose so," rejoined young Leland, with mock serious-
ness.

"Last summer," pursued Zeb, "when you's down de river
fishin', dere's thirteen of 'em come up one day to borrer de
wood-box.   I s'pose dey wanted to keep dar dogs and pap-
pooses in it, and I 'cluded as how dey warn't gwine to get it.
So I told 'em I's very sorry dat I couldn't 'commodate 'em,
but de fact war we wanted to put de wood in it ourselves.
When I said dat, one of de niggers begin to got sassy.   I just
informed 'em dat dey'd better make demselves scarce mighty
quick, if dey didn't want dis pusson in dar wool.   Dey didn't
mind what was said, howsumever, and purty soon I cotched
'em runnin' off wid de wood-box.   Dat raised my dander,
and I grabbed de box and frowed it right over dar heads and
cotched 'em fast.   Den I put a big stone on it, and kept 'em
dere free weeks, and afore I let 'em out I made 'em promise to
behave 'emselves.   Now I considers dat we'd better serve
'em some sich trick.   Tie two, free hundred to de fence, and
leave 'em dere for a few months."

"You are welcome to try it," returned George, rather disgusted at the negro's propensity for big story telling.   He
arose and passed within, where the ample table was laid.   Yet
he could not eat the plain, sweet food which Rosalind's own
hands had prepared.   The dreadful sense of danger was too
real a guest for any rest or peace of mind.

CHAPTER II.

THE NIGHT OF TERROR.

FEW words were interchanged during the evening. George and Rosalind had enough to occupy their minds, and Zeb, finding them taciturn, relapsed into a sullen silence.

At an early hour each retired. Rosalind now felt more than George that unaccountable presentiment which sometimes comes over one in cases of danger. During the last few hours it had increased until it nearly resolved itself into a certainty.

The view from the front of the house was clear and unobstructed to the river, a quarter of a mile distant. Along this lay the cultivated clearing, while the forest, stretching miles away, approached to within a few yards of the rear of the house.

Rosalind's room overlooked this wilderness. Instead of retiring, she seated herself by the window to gaze out upon it. There was a faint moon, and the tree-tops for a considerable distance could be seen swaying in the gentle night-wind. The silence was so profound that it seemed to make itself *felt* and, in that vast solitude few indeed could remain without being impressed with the solemn grandeur of nature around.

Hour after hour wore away; still Rosalind remained at the window. As there was no inclination to sleep, she determined to remain in her position until morning. She knew that it must be far beyond midnight, and at the thought there sprung up a faint hope within her breast. But she was startled by the dismal hoot of an owl. She sprung up, with a beating heart, listening intently and painfully; but no other sound was heard. Trying to smile at her trepidation, she again seated herself and listened; in a moment that cry was repeated, now in an opposite direction from which the first note was heard.

Rosalind wondered that the simple circumstance should so affect her; but try as much as she might, she could not shake it off. Again, for a few minutes, she remained trembling with an undefinable fear, when there came another hoot, followed instantly by another, in an opposite direction. She began now to entertain a fearful suspicion.

Her first impulse was to awaken her brother, but, after a moment's thought, she concluded to wait a short time. A few more sounds were heard, when they entirely ceased. During this time, Rosalind, although suffering an intense fear, had been gazing vacantly toward the point or clearing nearest the house. As her eyes rested upon the spot, she caught the shadowy outlines of a dark body moving stealthily and noiselessly along upon the ground.

Without waiting a moment, she darted to George's room. He had not slept, and in an instant was by her side.

" Call Zeb," she exclaimed. " We are surrounded by Indians."

Leland disappeared, and in a moment came back with the negro.

" Gorra mighty !" said the latter, in a hurried, husky whisper, " where am de cussed niggers ?   Heigh, Miss Rosa ?"

" Keep quiet," she replied, " or you will be heard."

" Dat's just what I wants to be, and I calkilates I'll be *felt* too, if dar are any of 'em 'bout."

" Stay here a moment," said George, " while I look out. Rosalind, what did you see ?"

" A body approaching the house from the woods.   Be careful and do not expose yourself, George."

He made no answer and entered her room, followed by herself and the negro, who remained at a safe distance, while he cautiously approached the window.   He had no more than reached it, when Zeb asked :

" See noffin' ?"

This question was repeated perhaps a dozen times without an answer, when the patience of Zeb becoming exhausted, he shuffled to the window and pressed his head forward, exclaiming :

" Gorra mighty, whar am dey ?"

" Hist ! there is one now—yes, two of them !"

" Whar—whar ?"

" Keep your mouth shut," interrupted the young man, his vexation causing him to speak louder than he intended.

"Heigh! dat's him! Look out!"

And before young Leland suspected his intentions or could prevent it, Zeb had taken aim and fired. This was so sudden, and unexpected that, for a moment, nothing was heard but the dull echo, rolling off over the forest and up the river. Then arose a piercing, agonized yell, that told how effectual was the shot of the negro. Rosalind's face blanched with terror as she heard the fearful chorus of enraged voices, and thought of the fearful scene that must follow.

"Are the doors secured?" she asked, laying her hand upon George's shoulder.

"Yes, I barricaded them all," he answered. "If they do not fire the building, we may be able to keep them off until morning. I don't know but what Zeb's shot was the best, after all—God save us!"

This last exclamation was caused by a bullet whizzing past, within an inch of his face. For a while Leland was uncertain of the proper course to pursue. Should he expose his person at the window, he was almost certain to be struck; yet this or some other one equally exposed, was the only place where he could exchange shots, and the savages must be kept in check.

Zeb had reloaded his gun, and peering around the edge of the window, caught a glimpse of an Indian. As reckless of danger as usual, he raised his rifle and discharged it. He was a good marksman, and the shot was as effective as the other.

"Gorra mighty!" he exclaimed, "I can dodge dar lead. Didn't I pick dat darkey off awful nice? Just wait till I load ag'in." Chuckling over his achievements, he proceeded to prime his rifle. George Leland withdrew to the window of another room, from which he succeeded in slaying a savage, and by being careful and cautious, he was able to make his few shots tell with effect.

When Zeb shot the first savage, the red-skins sprung to their feet and commenced yelling and leaping, feeling that those within were already at their mercy; but the succeeding shots convinced them of their mistake, and retreating to cover, they were more careful in exposing themselves. Several stole around to the front of the house, but George had anticipated them, and there being no means of concealing their appearance, they were easily kept at a distance. Rosalind followed and assisted him as far as lay in her power, while Zeb was left alone in his delight and glory.

"Be careful," said Leland; "don't come too near. Just have the powder and wadding ready and hand it to me when I need it."

"I will," she replied, in a calm, unexcited voice, as she reached him his rod.

"Just see what Zeb is at, while I watch my chance."

She disappeared, and in a moment returned.

"He seems frantic with delight, and is yet unharmed."

"God preserve him," said George, "for his assistance is needed."

"Be careful," said Rosalind, as George approached the window.

"I shall—whew! that's a close rub!" he muttered, as a bullet pierced his cap. "There, *you're* past harm," he added, as he discharged his gun.

Thus the contest was kept up for over an hour. But few shots were interchanged on either side, each party becoming more careful in their action. Young Leland remained at his window, and kept a close watch upon his field; but no human being was seen. Zeb laughed, ducked his head, and made numerous threats toward his enemies, but seemed to attract no notice from them.

Now and then Rosalind spoke a word to her brother, but the suspense which the silence of their enemies had put them in, sealed their lips, and, for a long while, the silence was unbroken by either. They were startled at length by the report of Zeb's rifle, and the next minute he appeared among them, exclaiming:

"Gorra mighty! I shot out my ramrod. I seen a good chance, and blazed away 'fore I thought to take it out. It went through six of 'em, and stuck into a tree and hung 'em fast. Heigh! it's fun to see 'em."

"Here, take mine, and for God's sake, cease your jesting!" said Leland, handing his rod to him.

"Wish I could string some more up," added Zeb, as he rammed home his charge. "Yer oughter seen it, Miss Rosa.

It went right frough de fust feller's eye, and den frough de oder one's foot, den frough de .oder's gizzard, and half way frough de tree. Gorra, how dey wriggled! Looked just like a lot of mackercl hung up to dry. Heigh!"

At this point Leland discharged his gun, and said, without changing his position:

"They are trying to approach the house. Go, Zeb, and attend to your side. Be very sharp!"

"Yes, I's dar, stringing 'em up," he rejoined, as he turned away.

"Hark!" exclaimed Rosalind, when he had gone. "What noise is that?"

Leland listened awhile, and his heart died within him as he answered:

"Merciful Heaven! the house is on fire! All hope is now gone!"

"Shall we give ourselves up?" hurriedly asked Rosalind.

"No; come with me."

"Hurry up, massa, dey's gwine to roast us. Dc grease begins to siss in my face a'ready," said Zeb, as he joined them.

The fugitives retreated to the lower story, and Leland led the way to a door which opened upon the kitchen, at the end of the house. His hope was that from this they might have a chance of escaping to the wood, but a short distance off, ere they were discovered.

Cautiously opening the door, he saw with anxious, hopeful joy, that no Indians were visible.

"Now, Rosalind," he whispered, "be quick. Make for the nearest trees, and if you succeed in reaching them, pass to the river-bank and wait for me. Move softly and rapidly."

Rosalind stepped quickly out. The yells of the infuriated savages deafened her; but, although fearfully near, she saw none, and started rapidly forward. Leland watched each step with an agony of fear and anxiety which can not be described. The trees were within twenty yards, and half the distance was passed, when Leland knew that her flight was discovered. A number of savages darted forward, but a shot from him stopped the course of the foremost. Taking advantage of the confusion which this had occasioned, Rosalind sprung away and

succeeded in reaching the cover; but here, upon the very
threshold of escape, she was reached and captured.

"Gorra mighty!" shouted Zeb, as he saw her seized and
borne away. "Ef I don't cowhide ebery nigger of 'em for dat
trick."

And clenching his hands he stalked boldly forward and demanded:

"Whar's dat lady? Ef you doesn't want to git into trouble,
I calkilate you'd better bring her back in double-quick time."

Several savages sprung toward him, and Zeb prepared himself for the struggle. His huge fist felled the first and the
second; but ere he could do further damage he found himself
thrown down and bound.

"Well, dar, if dat ain't de meanest trick yet, servin' a decent
prisoner dis way. I'll cowhide ebery one ob you. Oh, dear,
I wish I had de whip!" he muttered, writhing and rolling in
helpless rage upon the ground.

Leland had seen this occurrence and taken advantage of it.
It had served to divert the action of the savages, and the attention of all being occupied with their two prisoners, he
managed with considerable difficulty to reach the wood without being discovered.

Here, at a safe distance, he watched the progress of things.
The building was now one mass of flame, which lit up the sky
with a lurid, unearthly glare. The border of the forest was
visible and the trunks and limbs of the trees appeared as if
scorched and reddened by the consuming heat. The savages
resembled demons dancing and yelling around the ruin which
they had caused. It was with difficulty that Leland restrained
himself from firing upon them. With a sad heart he saw the
house which had sheltered him from infancy fall inward with
a crash. The splinters and ashes of fire were hurled in the
air and fell at his feet, and the thick volume of smoke reached
him.

Yet he thought more of the captives which were in the
hands of their merciless enemies. Their safety demanded his
attention. Thoughtfully and despondingly he turned upon
his heel and disappeared in the shadows of the great forest.

CHAPTER III.

KENT AND LESLIE.

WHEN Roland Leslie reached his destination some miles up the Ohio, his fears and suspicions were confirmed. There had been a massacre, a week previous, of a number of settlers, and the Indians were scouring the country for more victims.

This information was given by Kent Whiteman, the person for whom he was searching. This personage was a strange character, some forty years of age, who led a wandering hunter's life, and was known by every white man for a great distance along the Ohio. Roland Leslie had made his acquaintance when but a mere lad, and they often spent weeks together hunting and roaming through the great wilderness, which was the home of both. He cherished an implacable hatred to every red-man, and they in turn often sought his life, for they had no enemy so dangerous as he.

"Yes sir, them varmints," said he, as he leaned upon his long rifle and gazed at Leslie, "are playing particular devil in these parts, and I calkelate it's a game that two can play at."

"Jump in the boat, Kent," said Leslie, "and ride down with me; I promised George Leland that if he needed assistance I would bring it to him."

"He needs it, that's a p'inted fact, and as soon as it can conveniently reach him too."

"Well, let us be off." Leslie dipped his oars in the water and pulled out into the stream. It was the morning after the burning of the Lelands' home, which of course was unknown to them. For a few moments the boat glided rapidly down the stream, when Whiteman spoke:

"Where'd you put up last night, Leslie?"

"About ten miles down the river. I ran in under the bank and had an undisturbed night's rest."

"Didn't hear nothin' of the red-skins?"

"No."

"Wal, it's a wonder; they're as thick as flies in August, and I calkelate I'll have rich times with 'em."

"I can not understand how it is, Kent, that you cherish such a deadly hatred for these Indians."

"I have good reason," returned the hunter, compressing his lips.

"How long is it that you have felt thus?"

"Ever since I's a boy. Ever since *that* time."

"What time, Kent?"

"I have never told you, I believe, why the sight of a redskin throws me into such a fit, have I?"

"No; I should certainly be glad to hear."

"Wal, it doesn't take long to tell. Yet how few persons know it except myself. It is nigh thirty years ago," commenced Kent, "that I lived about a dozen miles above the place that we left this morning. There I was born and lived with my old father and mother until I was ten or eleven years old.

"One dark, stormy night we war attacked by them red devils, and that father and mother were butchered before my eyes. During the confusion of the attack, I escaped to the woods and secreted myself until it was over. It was a hard matter to lie there, scorched by the flames of your own home, and see your parents, while begging for mercy, tomahawked and slain before your eyes. But in such a position I was placed, and remained until the savages, satisfied with their bloody work, took their departure.

"When the rain, which fell in torrents, had extinguished the smoking ruins, I crawled from my hiding-place. I felt around until I come upon the cold bodies of my father and mother lyin' side by side, and then kneelin' over them, I took a fearful oath—an oath to which I have devoted my life. I swore that as long as life was given me, it should be used for revengin' the slaughter of my parents. That night these savages contracted a debt of which they little dreamed. Before they left the place, I had marked each of the dozen, and I never forgot them. For ten years I follered and tracked them, and at the end of that time I had sent the last one to his final account. Yet that did not satisfy me. I swore *eternal* enmity against the whole people, and as I said, it shall be carried out. While Kent is alive, he is the mortal enemy of very red-skin."

The hunter looked up in the face of Leslie, and his gleaming eyes and gnashing teeth told his earnestness. His manner and recital had impressed the latter, and he forbore speaking to him for some time.

"I should think," observed Leslie, after a short silence, "that you had nearly paid that debt, Kent."

"It is a debt which will be balanced," rejoined the hunter, "when I am unable to make any more payments."

"Well, I shouldn't want you for an enemy," added Leslie, glancing over his shoulder at the stream in front of him.

Both banks of the river at this point, and, in fact, for many miles, were lined with overhanging trees and bushes, which might afford shelter to any enemy. Kent sat in the stern and glanced suspiciously at each bank, as the boat was impelled swiftly yet silently forward, and there was not even a falling leaf that escaped his keen eye.

"Strikes me," said Leslie, leaning on his oars, "that we are in rather a dangerous vicinity. Those thick bushes along the shore, over there, might easily contain a few red gentlemen."

"Don't be alarmed," returned the hunter, "I'll keep a good watch. They've got to make some movement before they can harm us, and I'll be sure to see them. The river's wide, too, and there ain't so much to fear, after all."

Leslie again dipped his oars, and the boat shot forward in silence. Nothing but the suppressed dip of the slender ashen blades, or the dull sighing of the wind through the tree-tops, broke the silence of the great solitude. Suddenly, as Leslie bent forward and gazed into the hunter's face, he saw him start and gaze anxiously at the right shore, some distance ahead.

"What's the matter?" asked Leslie.

"Just wait a minute," returned the hunter, rising and gazing in the same direction. "Stop the boat. Back water!" he added, in a hurried tone.

Leslie did as he was bidden, and again spoke:

"What is it, Kent?"

"Do you see them bushes hangin' a little further out in the stream than the others?"

"Yes; what of them?"

"Watch them a minute. There—look quick !" said Kent.

"I can see a fluttering among the branches, as if a bird had flown from it," answered Leslie.

"Wal, them birds is Indians, that's all," remarked the hunter, dropping composedly back into the boat. "Go ahead !"

"They will fire into us, no doubt. Had I not better run in to the other shore ?"

"No; there may be a host of 'em there. Keep in the middle of the stream, and we'll give 'em the slip yet."

It must be confessed that Leslie experienced rather strange sensations as he neared the locality which had excited their suspicion, especially when he knew that he was exposed to any shot that they might feel inclined to give. A shudder ran through his frame, when, directly opposite the spot, he distinctly heard a groan of agony.

Kent made a motion for him to cease rowing. Bending their heads down and listening, they again heard that now loud, agonizing expression of mortal pain.

As soon as Leslie was certain that the sound proceeded from some being in distress, he headed the boat toward the shore.

"Stop !" commanded Kent; "you should have more sense than that."

"But will you not assist a person in distress ?" asked he, gazing reproachfully into his face.

"Who's in distress ?"

"Oh, Gorra mighty ! I's been dyin," now came from the shore.

"Hallo there ! what's wantin' ?" called Whiteman.

"Help, help, 'fore dis Indian gentleman—'fore I dies from de wounds dat dey's given me."

"I've heard that voice before," remarked Kent to Leslie, in an undertone.

"So have I," replied the latter. "Why, it is George Leland's negro; he wouldn't decoy us into danger. Let us go in."

"Wait until I speak further with him." (Then, to the person upon shore): "What might be your name ?"

"Zeb Langdon. Isn't dat old Kent?"

"Yes; how came you in this scrape, Zeb?"

"Gorra mighty! I didn't come into it. Dem red dogs —dese here nice fellers—brought me here 'bout two months ago, and den dey all fired at me fur two or free days, and den dey hung me up and left me to starve to death. Boo-hoo-oo!"

"But," said Leslie, "you were at home yesterday when I came up the river."

"Yes; dey burned down de house last night, and cooked us all and eat us up. I's come to live ag'in, and crawled down here to get you fellers to take me home; but, Lord bless you, don't come ashore—blast you, quit a hittin' me over de head," added the negro, evidently to some one near him.

Leslie and Whiteman exchanged significant glances, and silently worked the boat further from the land.

"Who is that you spoke to?" asked the former, when they were at a safe distance.

"Dis yere blasted limb reached down and pulled my wool," replied the negro, with perfect *nonchalance.*

"Where is George Leland?" asked Leslie.

"Dunno; slipped away from dese yere nice fellers what's pulled all de wool out of me head, and is tellin' me a lot o' yarns to tell you. Gorra mighty! can't you let a feller 'lone, when he's yarnin' as good as he can?"

"Where is Miss Leland?"

"How does I know? A lot of 'em run off wid her last night."

"Oh God! what I expected," said Leslie, dropping his voice, and gazing with an agonizing look at Whiteman. The latter, regardless of his emotion, continued his conversation with Zeb.

"Are you hurt any?"

"Considerable."

"Now, Zeb, tell the truth. Did they **capture** George Leland?"

"Bless you, no. He got away during de **trouble.**"

"Did they get Miss Leland?"

"'Deed they did."

"Is she with you?"

"No. It took forty of 'em to watch me and de rest."

Here the negro's words were cut short with a jerk, and he gave vent to a loud groan.

"Gorra mighty!" he ejaculated, in fury. "Come ashore, Mr. Whiteman and Mr. Leslie. Come quick, and let dese yer fellers got you. Dey wants yer too."

"Are there any of the imps with you?" asked Kent, more for amusement than any thing else.

"What shall I tell him?" the negro asked, in a husky whisper, loud enough to be plainly heard by the two in the boat.

"Dey say dar ain't any of 'em. Talk yourself, if dat doesn't suit you," he added, in great wrath.

"Three cheers for you," shouted Whiteman. "Are there any of 'em upon the other side?"

"Dese fellers say dey am all dar. Gorra, don't kill me."

"Good; you're the best nigger 'long the 'Hio. I guess we'll go over to the other side and visit them."

So saying, Kent seized the oars and pulled for the opposite shore. He had not taken more than a couple of strokes when a dozen rifles cracked simultaneously from the bushes, and as many bullets struck the boat and glanced over the water.

"Drop down," he whispered to Leslie. Instead of doing the same himself, he bent the more vigorously to his oars. A few minutes sufficed to carry them so far down that little danger was to be apprehended from the Indians, who uttered their loudest shouts and discharged their rifles, as they passed beyond their reach.

"That's too good a chance to be lost," muttered the ranger, bringing his long rifle to his shoulder. Leslie followed the direction of his aim, and saw a daring savage standing boldly out to view, and making furious gesticulations toward them. The next instant Kent's rifle uttered it's sharp report, and the Indian, with a yell, sprung several feet in the air, and fell to the ground.

"That was a good shot," remarked Leslie, gazing at the fallen body.

"Yes, and it's done just what I wanted it to," replied Kent, heading the boat toward shore.

"They are going to pursue us, are they not?" asked Leslie.

"Yes, and we'll have fun," added the ranger, as the boat touched the shore, and he sprung out.

"Come along, and make up yer mind for a long run," said he, glancing furtively toward the savages.

Leslie sprung after him, and they darted away into the forest.

When Whiteman had fired his fatal shot the Indians were so infuriated, that, setting up their demoniac yells, they plunged down the banks of the stream, determined to revenge their fallen companion.

This was what Kent desired. He exulted as he saw that he was being gratified. "If there isn't fun pretty shortly it won't be my fault," said he, as he plunged onward into the forest.

In a short time the pursuers gained the opposite shore, and followed with renewed ardor into the wilderness. Kent and Leslie, however, had gained a good start. Both being rapid runners, they had not much to fear. Had nothing unusual occurred, they would easily have distanced their pursuers. But Leslie, following Kent in a leap across a rocky gorge, struck in his comrade's footsteps in the earth upon its edge. The earth had become loosened and started by the shock, and ere Leslie could recover his footing, he fell some fifteen or twenty feet to the bottom. The fall bruised him so much that he was unable to rise, or in fact hardly to stir.

"Hurt?" asked the ranger, gazing over at him.

"Yes," groaned Leslie. "I can't get up. Don't wait for me, for it's no use. Go on and save yourself."

"I hate to leave you, but it's got to be done. Lay down there; crawl in under that rock. Perhaps they won't see you. Quick, for I hear 'em comin'."

With these words the hunter turned and disappeared, and succeeded in getting beyond the gorge without being seen by his pursuers; but this delay had given them time to gain a great deal upon him, and when he started their hurried tramp could be distinctly heard.

His words had roused Leslie to a sense of his peril. By

struggling and laboring for a few minutes he succeeded in disengaging himself and managed to crawl beneath a projecting ridge of rock. This effectually concealed him from sight ·' and had his pursuers no suspicion of his fall, he yet stood chance of escaping.

In a few moments he heard them overhead, and the pain' of his wounds was forgotten in the anxiety which he now felt for his safety. He knew that they had hesitated, but whether it was on account of the leap which they were required to make, or on account of any suspicion that they might entertain, he could not divine.

The place in which he had fallen had probably once been swept by a torrent, but now a tiny stream only warbled through it. The murmur of this, by Leslie's side, prevented his understanding the words of those above. The hum of their voices could be heard but not their words.

Presently, however, he distinguished a well-known voice evidently in expostulation with some one.

"Gorra mighty! does yer s'pects I can jump dat? It's bad 'nough to make me git drownded in dat river without broken my neck down dar!"

Leslie could not help wondering why Zeb was brought along, nor how he managed to keep pace with the rest. But as he had not heard his voice before, he concluded that the negro must have been brought by several Indians who remained behind for that purpose. This conclusion was confirmed by the words which he heard the next minute.

"Whar's de use ob jumpin'? Dem yere fellers 'll soon be back, coz dey ain't agwine to cotch dat man nohow. He can run like a streak o' sunshine, and likes as not dey'll all get shot. You'd better go on and coax 'em to come back while I stay here and waits fur ye."

In answer to this, Leslie heard some angry muttering and mumbling, but could distinguish no words. In a moment, however, Zeb's voice was audible.

"Bless yer, you're de all-firedest fools I eber see'd. How does you s'pects I's gwine to light on toder side. Ef one of you'll take me on your back, I won't mind lettin' you try to carry me over; but I tells you I ain't agwine to try it. So you can shut up yer rat-traps."

Hardly a second elapsed before he again spoke :

" Hold on dar ; you kickin' all my brains out ! I'll try it !"

The next moment Leslie heard a dull thump, and Zeb came ,olling down directly beside him.

" I's killed !   Ebery bone is broken.   I can't live anoder second."

" Zeb ! Zeb !" whispered Leslie, in a hurried whisper.

The negro suddenly ceased his groaning and exclamations, and rolling his head over toward him, asked, in a whisper :

" Who's dat ?"

" It's I, Zeb.   Get up quick, for God's sake, before they come down, or I'm lost !"

The negro clambered to his feet without difficulty, and disappeared, shouting to those above :

" I isn't hurt.   It war de rock dat was broke by my head striking it !   How de pieces flewed !"

CHAPTER IV

THE CAPTIVES.

WHEN Rosalind Leland felt herself seized by the savage, she fainted in the arms of her swarthy captor, and so remained for a long space of time.   When she recovered, she found that she was a secure prisoner in the hands of her enemies. She was grieved to see that Zeb was a companion in captivity.   She felt that, could she alone suffer, she would willingly bear it.   Although acquainted with many Indians, she was unable to recognize any of those around.   This, of course, was a gratification.   It showed that the kindness of her par ents and herself had not been lost upon them.   Although the recipients of her kindness might not strive to prevent violence being done her, yet they refused to participate in it themselves.

The whole Indian force numbered about thirty.   As soon as they had done all in their power, and were convinced that there were no more captives to be secured, they took up the ,ine of march.   In the course of their journey, Rosalind found

that she was near enough to hold a conversation with Zeb, and
after a few minutes' silence, she ventured :

"How do you feel, Zeb?"

"Bless you, missus, if dese niggers doesn't get the all-firedest walloping when I gets de chance, dey may feel glad."

"Yes, but I am afraid that you will not get the chance very
soon."

"Oh, dey daresn't kill me; fur if dey did, I'd hang ebery
one ob dem."

Despite Rosalind's painful situation, she could not but smile
at the earnestness of tone in which Zeb delivered himself of
this. She resumed :

"Are you bound, Zeb?"

"Not much ; only a dozen ropes tied around one leg, and
as many round de rest ob me body."

"Oh, Zeb, don't tell such stories."

"Fact, missus Leland. I counted 'em when dey's puttin'
'em on, and dey cut like forty, too."

"Forty-two what?" asked a gruff voice by Zeb's side, in
very good English.

"Gorra mighty, *who's dat?*"

No answer was given.

"Who de debbil was dat?" asked Zeb, speaking to Rosalind.

She made no answer and appeared to be lost in a reverie.
Zeb repeated his question but failed to elicit any reply. Muttering something to himself, he permitted her silence to remain
undisturbed.

There were two horses in the party, and upon one of these
Rosalind had been placed. The other was bestrode by a savage, who appeared to be the leader of the band. Zeb's hands
were pinioned behind his back, and he was compelled to walk
behind the horse of Rosalind, with a guard that kept a close
eye upon his movements.

Silently yet rapidly the body moved along through the forest of impenetrable darkness, where a perfect knowledge was
required in order to make the least progress. Rosalind's horse
was a powerful creature, and carried her with comparative
comfort. Now and then the cold leaves brushed her face, or
her body grazed some tree, yet the animal carried her safely

and unharmed. Several times the thought of escape flashed upon her. It seemed easy to turn her horse's head and gallop beyond the reach of her enemies. But one of them was mounted, and she believed she could elude him. She could ride down those immediately around her, and what was there to prevent her making good her escape?

And yet, after a few more minutes of thought, she abandoned all hopes of liberty for the present. Her brother was free, and would leave no means untried until she was again restored to him; and there was *another one*, who, she knew in her heart, would exert himself to the utmost to save her. This thought caused her heart to beat faster and faster. There was a slight tremor in her voice as she spoke:

"Zeb, come a little nearer to me."

He made a movement, but was unable to approach much nearer.

"Are you listening?" she asked, in a subdued tone.

"Yes, missus; mouth, ears and eyes is open."

"Then," said she, bending toward him and lowering her voice still more, "I wish to ask you, Zeb, whether you would do me a favor?"

"Lord bless you, missus, you knows I'd die a hundred times for you."

"I believe you would," returned Rosalind, touched by his tone and words; "but it is no hardship that I ask of you."

"Well, out with it quick, fur dese fellers don't like to see yer horse's side rubbin' all de wool off ob my head."

"You are acquainted with Roland Leslie, Zeb?" asked Rosalind, bending lower and speaking in a whisper which she scarcely heard herself.

"Yes," answered Zeb, breathing hurriedly.

"Well, should you see him, tell him of my situation; and—and—tell him not to run into danger for my sake."

"I will," rejoined Zeb, fervently.

Here a savage, judging that matters had gone far enough, jerked the negro rudely back.

"You needn't be so spiteful," retorted Zeb; "she's told me all she's agwine to."

Rosalind had done so; nothing further passed between them.

Toward morning they reached the banks of a stream, where the savages divided into two parties. The one which retained the negro started down the Ohio, while those who held Rosalind continued their journey in a southerly direction.

The course of the former has already been given, and also a part of their doings. The latter, which numbered twenty, experienced nothing worthy of record for a considerable time. They moved forward rapidly, as they had some fears of pursuit. This was their reason for retaining Rosalind with them. They were cunning enough to know that what efforts might be made would be for her sake, while probably the negro would be left to himself.

Their progress south continued until Rosalind knew that she was many miles in Kentucky. They had kept along the banks of a river during the whole time, which she also knew to be the Big Sandy. From this she judged that her captors were a tribe, or at least a part of one, which belonged many miles distant from where her home had been.

Throughout all her trials, Rosalind relied upon Providence with a firm, unshaken faith. Although hope dawned but faintly upon her, she murmured not. Her fears were great for others beside herself. She was young, and her youthful blood coursed through her veins, bearing with it the pleasures and hopes of life just commenced. It was hard to die, hard to give up the hopes which had only begun to dawn in her bosom ; yet, if it was His will, she felt that she could go without a murmur. " Thy will be done," was the prayer which but herself and Heaven heard.

CHAPTER V

THE MEETING ON THE RIVER.

FOR some minutes after Zeb's disappearance, Leslie remained without moving, scarcely breathing for fear there might still be some Indians overhead; but as minute after minute wore by, and no sound above warned him that his enemies were in the vicinity, he managed to creep from his hiding-place and seat himself upon a rock near by.

Now that he was safe for the present, he began to examine his wounds. There being no strong emotion to occupy his mind, the pain again came upon him, and he feared that he might be dangerously hurt; but, upon examination he was gratified to see that he was only bruised in two or three places. In falling, he had first struck upon his feet; his side, from the force of the concussion, came rather violently in contact with the jagged, projecting rocks. This gave a few severe flesh-cuts, which, for the time being, were more painful and distressing than would have been a wound of a more serious character.

Still, he found that he was unable to walk without great labor and pain, and concluded to remain in his present position until morning. He crawled back into the hiding-place, and disposed of himself for the night. Little sleep, however, was gained, and the night seemed the longest that he had ever spent.

When morning dawned, he emerged from his hard resting-place, and, with great difficulty, made his way to the top. Then, shaping his course toward the river, he reached it in the course of an hour or so. Here, to his great joy, he found the boat that he and Kent had left. It was pulled high and dry upon the bank, yet he succeeded in getting it in the water, and, with a light heart, pushed out from the shore.

It was so much easier to propel the boat than to walk, that he had no difficulty in making good headway. He had determined upon no course to pursue, but continued moving forward with a sort of instinct, hardly caring in what direction he went. He was moving toward the spot where once the house of the Lelands stood ; some impulse seemed drawing him thitherward.

The truth was, Roland Leslie was thinking of Rosalind and her situation. Although he had spoken to her but comparatively a few times, yet those occasions had awakened a feeling in his breast which he found could not be subdued ; his love was growing day by day. He knew not whether she was aware of his passion, but his fluttering heart told him, at least, that she had not frowned upon him.

Young love rests upon the slightest foundation ; thus Leslie was encouraged and made hopeful by the remembrance of the friendly meeting which he had with Rosalind. Then, as he awoke from this pleasant reverie into which he had fallen, the consciousness that she was now a captive among the Indians, the thought maddened him. He dipped his oars deep in the water, and moved swiftly along.

It occurred to him that perhaps it would be best to keep a watch of the shores ahead, to prevent running carelessly into danger. There might be Indians concealed or lurking in the vicinity, and he would be easily drawn into a decoy, should he be careless and thoughtless.

He turned around and scanned the shore more closely and searchingly. Seeing nothing suspicious, he was about to resume rowing again, when, from an overhanging cluster of bushes came the sharp crack of a rifle, and a bullet split one of the oars, a few inches below his hand. Seizing his rifle, he turned toward the point from which the shot had come, but could see no person. The thin wreath of smoke curling slowly up from the bushes showed the point from which it had been given ; but whoever the person might be, he kept himself well concealed. In a moment another shot was given, which glanced over the water a few feet from the stern.

Leslie began to think that he was in rather a close situation, and clutching his rifle nervously, endeavored to ascertain the point from which the shot had come, determined to return one at all hazards. He did not dare to pass over to the opposite side, for he had a suspicion that they were intended for that purpose. He believed that his person had not been aimed at, but the balls had been intended to pass closely enough to alarm him and cause him to seek safety by pulling for the other shore, where, probably, a foe was waiting. While he sat undetermined what course to pursue, a form stepped out in full view upon the bank, and accosted him.

"Frightened any ?"

"Well, I should think I ought to be. Why, is that you, George ?"

"I believe so. Come in and take me aboard."

"What reason had you for firing upon me ?" asked Leslie approaching him.

"Well, not any. I saw you coming down-stream, and an idea seized me to learn if you were easily frightened."

"I felt rather nervous when that shot came," returned Leslie, pointing at the hole in his oar.

"It was a close rub ; but, of course, I took good care not to make it too close."

"What is the news? What reason have you for being here ?" asked Leslie, interrupting him.

"News enough," returned Leland, gloomily.

"Step in the boat and let me hear it."

As they passed down-stream, Leland narrated his story, and when he had finished, remarked :

"Roland, I have sought you for advice and assistance, and I trust both will be given me."

"Gladly ! Do you think, George, that I could rest as long as your sister is in the hands of those savages ?"

"Pardon me," returned Leland, "if I at all doubted. This affliction weighs heavily upon me."

"I suspected this state of things," continued Leslie, "and it is the reason that I hurried down-stream. Yet the uncertainty of seeing you or any friend, deterred me from making haste to your place."

Here Leslie gave the circumstances of his encountering Zeb, and his subsequent misfortune, or, as he termed it, his fortune, of falling in the gorge.

"Then Kent is gone, is he ?" asked George, when he had finished. "That is too bad, for we need his assistance greatly."

"In fact, I do not understand what we shall be able to do without him," added Leslie.

"Nor I; and here we are as helpless as if we were already in the hands of the Indians, so far as regards any assistance that we can give Rosalind," continued Leland.

"Oh, don't despair so soon. I trust that Kent will soon turn up, and we shall then have a good chance to recover her."

"Where do you suppose that Kent can be?"

"I can only guess."

"What reason have you then for thinking that we shall meet him?"

"This reason. He saw me fall, and was obliged to leave me for a time, as the pursuers were close at hand. I am certain that, as soon as he eluded and escaped them, he would return to the place for me."

"And find you gone and give you up."

"No; he would search the place, and seeing my trail, would follow it. I left a pretty plain one, and he will meet with no difficulty."

"But suppose the ranger is captured himself?"

"There is no supposition in the case," rejoined Leslie, with an air of assurance.

"Well, admitting what you say," continued Leland, "did you leave a trail after getting in the boat, that will be easy for him to follow?"

"Easy enough. He knows what course I would take, and, consequently, he knows what one to pursue."

"But, even then, can he overtake you?"

"I have not come very rapidly, and I think that he can. I believe that at this moment he is on the way."

"Well, Roland, we have probably speculated enough upon our chances of meeting him. In the mean time, what do you propose that we do with ourselves?"

"As to that, I am hardly decided. There is great danger in our remaining on the river, and yet I see no means which will be so apt to bring us in communication with Kent."

"This gliding down the Ohio in broad daylight, when we know the woods on both sides are full of our enemies, is rather dangerous business, although it may possess some advantages for us."

"I leave the matter with you," said Leslie. "The stream is very broad for a considerable distance, and both of us ought to understand enough of wood-craft to prevent running into danger."

"We *ought* to understand enough," said Leland, significantly, "but the fact is, we do *not*. There are so many contrivances these cunning rascals devise for a white man's destruction, that one needs to have a schooling of years in their ways to understand them. However," he added, in a whisper, "I understand *that* contrivance yonder."

"What is that?" inquired his companion, in some excitement.

"Take a careful look down-stream and tell me whether you see any thing unusual."

"No—I don't know as I do," slowly repeated Leslie. "Hold on—yes I do—yonder is a log, or more likely two or three of them—a raft. I suppose, Leland, it is for our benefit."

"Undoubtedly. It was constructed for the benefit of the white race generally; and, as we come first we are to be served first."

"Let us cut in to shore and give them the slip."

"It may be the very thing they wish us to do. The action of the savages, so far, shows that they are more anxious to take prisoners than to slay men. So keep quiet and don't allow yourself to become nervous."

CHAPTER VI.

THE RAFT.

SLOWLY, silently and gently the boat glided onward—both Leslie and Leland as motionless as death, yet with hearts throbbing wildly and fearfully. The former stooped and whispered :.

"There are three Indians on it, upon the opposite side from us. We must pass beyond the log before they will be in range of our guns. They will not fire until we begin to pass them. Take a quick but sure aim, and drop down in the bottom of the boat the instant your gun is discharged."

Nearer and nearer came the canoe to the log, until but a

few rods separated them, but not a breath or fluttering of a leaf disturbed the profound silence.

When at the nearest point, scarcely more than two rods would separate them. Still onward the boat swept until its prow was even with the log.

"Ready," whispered Leslie, "you take the nearest one."

The next instant the enemies were in full view of each other. Simultaneously the two rifles in the boat broke the solemn stillness. But not a sound showed whether their shots had produced any effect at all! Not a savage's head, however, could be seen! They either had been slain or else had quietly drawn out of sight when they became aware of the danger that menaced them. The latter was most probably the case, although neither of the whites could satisfy himself upon that point.

As the thin haze from the guns diffused itself over the spot, the same oppressive silence settled upon the water, and the same absence of life was manifest in every thing around. So sudden had been the interruption, that, a few minutes afterward, it was almost impossible to realize that it had actually occurred. More than once both Leslie and Leland caught themselves debating this very point in their minds.

For a few moments the two remained concealed within the boat, for they well knew that danger yet threatened; but, nervously excited over the event, Leland, with a sad want of discretion, peered over the gunwale of the canoe.

"Down, instantly," admonished his companion, catching his shoulder.

The report of another gun came at that very instant, and George dropped so suddenly and awkwardly out of sight, that Leslie inquired with much concern:

"Are you hurt?"

"Pretty near it, at any rate," returned Leland, putting his hand to his face.

He was not struck, however, although the ball had grazed and marked his cheek. The instant Leland saw that he was not injured, he raised himself and aimed toward the log. No sign of an enemy was visible, and not knowing but what there might be more loaded rifles behind the contrivance, he dropped his head again.

Peering cautiously over the gunwale, the young man saw the raft gradually approaching the Kentucky shore. The Indians possessing no means of reloading their pieces without running great risk, probably deemed it best to make a safe retreat.

The distance between the whites and the savages slowly but surely increased, and when the former judged they were comparatively safe, they arose and plied their paddles.

"Now if we can only come across Kent, I shall be pretty hopeful of getting out of the woods," remarked Leslie.

"But how is that to be done? There is just the trouble."

"I think he will find us if we only wait for him."

"I agree with you, that it is all that we can do. We will row down-stream a short distance further, where we will be sheltered more from the observation of our enemies, and wait until he comes, or until it is pretty certain that he will not."

Leslie bent to his oars, and the boat again shot forward. Each now felt a stronger hope. The depression of spirits under which Leland was laboring began to undergo a reaction.

Leslie was naturally of a more buoyant disposition than Leland, and seldom suffered those spells of melancholy which are so apt to affect those of a temperament less sanguine. The latter at seasons was more light-hearted than the former, yet adverse circumstances easily affected and depressed him.

The locality to which Leslie had referred was a place in the river where the overhanging boughs and underwood were so thick and luxuriant that it was an easy matter to send a small boat beneath them and remain effectually hidden from any enemy passing up or down the river.

Their plan was to conceal themselves, and thus, while affording themselves comparative security, to keep an unremitting watch for the appearance of Kent. They expected, and in fact were certain, that he would descend the opposite side, which, from their hiding-place, could be easily seen.

Leslie, with a vigorous pull, sent the boat under the sweeping branches, and, coming to rest, remarked:

"There, George, we are safe for the present. An Indian might pass within twenty feet of us, and not dream of our proximity."

"True, Leland, I feel glad that we are thus fortunate."

"See," continued Leslie, "what a nice arrangement. From my seat I can keep a good view of the opposite side."

"How long do you intend to remain here?" asked Leland, whose fears were ever on the alert.

"Can't say precisely."

"Remember that food will be necessary, and soon necessary, too."

"I am aware of that, yet we can do without it for some time. If Kent is going to pass us, it will be during to-morrow."

"Leslie," said Leland, earnestly, "I have been thinking deeply upon our chances of meeting him, and I must confess that they seem few indeed."

"I do not doubt it. They would have the same appearance to me, were it not for one thing. I have been calculating, and though, of course, a great deal of guess-work has been employed, yet I think that I have come to a very nearly correct conclusion. I'm pretty positive that if Kent reaches us, it will be in the neighborhood of to-morrow at mid-day. Not seeing him, I shall fire my rifle. Kent knows the sound of it, and will search for us."

"Perhaps he may not be upon the opposite shore."

"Which will be as well, yet I can think of no reason that would induce him to cross."

"In the mean time, how do you propose that we pass away time and keep off *ennui.*"

"In sleep, if that is possible."

"I think it is with myself," returned Leland, with a light laugh.

"And the same with me," added Leslie.

"Well, the circumstances being favorable, I propose that we commence operations at once."

"A good suggestion."

Both disposed themselves as best they could in the boat, and being tired and fatigued, were soon asleep.

CHAPTER VII

LOST AND FOUND.

THE two young men slept soundly through the night. When Leslie awoke it was broad day, and his companion was still asleep. He suffered him to remain so until the day was well advanced. Then each felt the pangs of hunger. Leland proposed that one should land and go in quest of food, but Leslie answered:

"If Kent appears, it will be in the course of a few hours. We had better wait and see what comes of patience."

Another hour of silence wore away. Leland was about to speak when Leslie exclaimed, in a whisper:

"Hush!"

They listened intently. In a moment the steady, measured dip of paddles could be heard. Whoever was approaching had little fear or apprehension of danger; for they came fearlessly along, and were moving with considerable noise and swiftness.

Leland and Leslie held their breath as the sound came steadily nearer. Not a whisper was exchanged. The former, from his position, could not discern any object that might be passing, but the latter had a full view of the river.

In a moment the whole force passed before Leslie's eyes. Two canoes loaded with Indians glided past, unconscious of their proximity. Each drew a long breath of relief; but for a considerable time neither ventured a whisper.

"It appears to me that Indians are plenty in these parts," remarked Leland.

"Rather more than I could wish," returned his companion.

"Confound it, it will soon be time to fire your gun, and of course the savages will hear it."

"But for all that I shall risk it. It will not do to let Kent escape us."

"How soon do you intend discharging your piece?"

"In an hour or so."

"Well, see here, Roland, if Kent comes, it can not be

expected that he will have any food. The report of your gun
will doubtless reach the ears of enemies as well as friends."

"I expect it will."

"And still further: if such be the case, we shall not dare
to land for fear of an encounter. We may be obliged to remain concealed for a few days, and no means will be left to
procure food during that time. Now, what I am coming at
is this : while we have an opportunity to get it, let us do it."

"How do you propose obtaining it ?"

"Easily enough. Just let me land, and I will insure you
success in a short time."

"But you have overlooked one thing."

"What is it ?"

"The report of your gun will be heard as well as mine,
and will be as likely to attract the attention of any enemies in
the neighborhood."

"That is true, but I can reach the boat in time."

"And although Kent is within a short distance, I shall not
dare to apprise him of our situation."

"Such appears to be the case; but you must see that it is
absolutely necessary that *some* means should be taken to secure
food."

"I admit it, and am willing that you should try."

"Hold !" exclaimed Leland, brightening up. "I have a
plan. You say that Kent, in the course of an hour or so, will
probably be near enough for you to fire. I will try and not
bring down any game until that time, and the minute you
hear the report of my gun you must discharge yours. This
will have the effect that you wish, and I shall have time to
reach you before any one can come up."

"A capital idea," said Leslie. "Hearing two guns, the
Indians will have a little more fear in approaching us, than
they would did they hear but one You deserve credit,
George, for the thought."

"Remember, and wait until you hear my gun, before you
fire yours," replied he.

"I will wait an hour, George ; and then, whether I hear
yours or not, I shall discharge mine. As I said awhile ago,
it won't do to let Kent escape us, and I must be sure to warn
him."

"I trust that I shall encounter game before that time, but should I not, you must do as you said. I will return upon hearing you."

"And return instantly," said Leslie, impressively. "Don't wait until the danger is increased. Although it may seem that a few minutes will enable you to procure abundant food, don't wait a single minute. It may cost you your life, if you do."

"I will remember your advice. Now shove in a little nearer shore and I will be off."

Leslie brought the boat to the bank, and Leland stepped off.

"Try and not be gone long; do not wander too far, for it will be an easy thing to get lost in this forest. Remember that it will take you considerable time to reach me, and if the distance be too great, an enemy may be ahead of you. Be careful in all your movements, and be sure to return the instant that my gun is heard."

"I will try and obey you," returned Leland. And George disappeared in the mazes of the woods.

Leslie returned to his former position, and more to occupy his mind than any thing else, gazed out upon the broad bosom of the Ohio, as it glided majestically along, through the dark shadows of the forest. It then presented a far different appearance from what it does at this day. No crowded cities then lined its banks. The flaming steamboat had not broken its surface; the canoe, gliding noiselessly over it, was all that gave token of the presence of man. A rude cabin erected in some lone spot in the wilderness, like a green spot in the desert, showed the feeble footing which he had upon the soil.

Solemnly and silently the old Ohio rolled along through its hundreds of miles until it as solemnly and silently united with the great father of waters.

When one has recently passed through an exciting and momentous occurrence, and is then left completely alone, it is difficult to keep from falling into a reverie; the subject which interests the mind most will finally occupy it to the exclusion of every thing else.

Thus it was with Roland Leslie. At first he began speculating upon the probable success of Leland's enterprise; then upon the probability of his arresting the attention of Kent, should he chance to be in the vicinity. Having considered this for some time, he reflected upon the dangers through which he had passed, and upon the likelihood of further deliverance from them. This thought called to mind his mishap among the rocks, and he proceeded to examine his wounds, of which, for some time, he had entirely ceased to think. These being not very severe, as we have shown, had failed to trouble him, and he was glad to see that they needed no more attention.

Again left to his thoughts, they shortly wandered to Rosalind Leland. Where was she? Was she alive, or already slain? Was there any hope of meeting her again? Could *he* do any thing toward rescuing her from bondage? He felt certain that she was alive, although a close prisoner, and was confident that recovery was possible. That he determined she *should be* rescued, and that he should be the one that would do it, was not strange.

Love will upset the mind of any person, and at times play the *wild* with him. Leslie was naturally clear-headed, far-sighted and sagacious; yet, when he permitted his ideas to dwell upon the object of his love, they sadly misused him. At such times he was another person. He lost sight of the obstacles and dangers which would have been apparent to any one gifted with ordinary shrewdness; and he formed plans which, in his sober moments, would have only excited his ridicule.

Strange as it may seem for such a person to have been guilty of such an idea, Leslie had not pondered upon the absorbing topic for any length of time before he deliberately came to the conclusion to rescue Rosalind in the course of three days, to rebuild her old home, and settle down with her for the rest of his life! Of course the savages would never disturb him, and he should be, without doubt, the happiest mortal in existence!

He was suddenly awakened from his reverie by the faint report of Leland's rifle. It sounded fully a mile distant, and the certainty of his danger made him tremble with apprehension. George, as he feared, had forgotten the warning given him, and, in the excitement, had unconsciously wandered to a greater distance than he supposed. In all probability he was lost, and would be obliged to seek the river and follow it in order to find Leslie. This would require time, and he had already exposed himself to danger by firing his gun.

Although Roland had promised to fire upon hearing Leland, yet he forebore to do it. The difference which a half-hour would make in the probability of Kent's hearing his own gun, would be in his favor. He supposed that Leland, upon discharging his piece, had instantly set out to return, and he wished to give him almost sufficient time to reach him.

Anxiously and painfully Roland listened, with his finger upon the trigger of his gun; and, as minute after minute wore away without a sound reaching him, he began to hope that Leland could be at no great distance.

A few more minutes were passed, when Roland concluded that the time for firing his signal had arrived. It would serve to guide Leland, and, had he not deceived himself, would reach the ears of Kent. Standing up in the boat, he raised the gun above his head, and was already pressing the trigger, when he paused, as he heard the sharp crack of Leland's rifle at no great distance. He waited a few seconds, until the echo had died away, and then discharged his own.

He remained stationary a moment, as though to permit the sound to escape entirely from his rifle. Then, reseating himself, proceeded to reload it. This done, he impatiently listened for a returning signal. He had placed a great deal of reliance and hope upon that shot, and, as he now was so soon to learn whether it had accomplished what he wished, he could not keep down his fearful anxiety.

He was nervous, and listened with painful interest for the slightest sound. The falling of a leaf startled him ; and, at last, unable to restrain himself, he determined again to fire his gun.

At that instant there came a crash of Leland's rifle, followed by the maddened shouts of infuriated savages, so near that Leslie sprung to his feet and gazed about him. Recovering himself, he stooped, and, seizing a paddle, began shoving the boat toward shore, fully determined to afford his friend all the assistance that lay in his power.

. The boat had hardly touched, when there was a rustling in the bushes directly before him, and the next instant Kent stood beside him.

"Quick—shove out! They arc after me!" he exclaimed, springing into the boat and grasping the oars

"Where is George?" asked Leslie.

"They've got him, and came nigh getting me. Cuss the infernal devils!"

In a moment the two had freed themselves from the bushes. As the yells of their enemies were heard upon the shore, they had reached the center of the stream, and were passing swiftly downward.

CHAPTER VIII.

THE COMPANION IN CAPTIVITY.

WHEN Leland left the boat, he wandered forward for a considerable distance, not noticing the direction in which he was going, only intent upon securing game of some sort of other. Still, he exercised considerable caution in his movements, and determined not to risk a shot unless he was certain of his success. Birds and quadrupeds were plenty, and he did not entertain any doubts of his ability to secure all that he wished. He permitted several good shots to pass, for the reason that he did not wish to fire until the hour was up. By this means he unconsciously increased the distance between himself and Leslie, until it occurred to him that the hour had nearly expired. A few minutes after, having a good opportunity, he improved it, and, securing his prize, turned to retrace his steps.

Then it flashed upon him, for the first time, that he was lost. As we said, he had failed to notice the direction, and had no idea of the course to pursue in order to reach the river. The only means left was to proceed by guess; contrary to what might be expected, he took the right course. His anxiety caused him to be somewhat heedless; and after proceeding a short distance, he again discharged his rifle. Then hearing the report of Leslie's rifle but a short distance away, he set joyously forward, confident of soon coming up to him. He had not gone far when he heard a suppressed, significant whistle. Hardly conscious of its meaning, he paused and listened. It was repeated, and becoming suspicious, he sprung behind a tree. While listening, the subdued voice of Kent reached him :

"Make for the river, George; the imps are on your trail."

He turned to obey this injunction, but had not taken a dozen steps when a rifle flamed from some concealment, and a twinge in his side told him that he was wounded. At the same instant several savages sprung toward him, setting up their demoniac howls. The pain of his wound maddened him, and, regardless of consequences, he raised his rifle and shot the foremost through the breast, when scarcely the length of his gun from him.

This act, though rash, and one which he would not have done in his cooler moments, was the means eventually of saving his life. The intention of the savages was to kill him on the spot; but the death of one of their number increased their fury and thirst for vengeance, and the chief or leader deterred the others from further violence, determined that his death should be at the stake.

"You shoot Indian, eh ?" said one, through his closed teeth, brandishing his knife at the same time in the face of the young man.

He made no reply; but weakened by the loss of blood, sunk fainting to the ground. He was jerked to his feet, and although barely able to stand, was forced forward, and compelled to keep pace with the others.

The Indians who had thus captured Leland were the same band who had pursued him and Kent. The latter had taken a circuitous course, and, after placing a considerable distance between himself and his enemies, took the back track and reached the gorge where Leslie had fallen, hoping to find him there; but being disappointed, followed his trail to the river where he saw that he had embarked in the boat.

Kent knew that his own trail would be followed. In order to mislead the savages, he took to the water and swam about a half-mile down-stream before he landed upon the opposite side. But it seemed that fate was against him. The savages in pursuing him had separated somewhat. Kent's ruse one of them accidentally discovered, and apprised his companions. They collected and immediately took the right trail. The first intimation the ranger had of his danger was the whistling of a bullet a few inches from his head, as he was nearing the bank ; and when his feet rested upon land, his unwearied and tenacious enemies were in the river, boldly crossing toward him.

When the Indians reached the bank, Kent was already at a great distance, yet they continued their pursuit, and had gone some distance, when the first report of Leland's rifle reached their ears. This they mistook for Kent's, and abandoning the trail, made directly toward it. The second discharge of the young man's gun occurred when he was but a short distance from them. Kent endeavored to warn him of his danger, but as we have seen, it was too late. He himself was discovered and hotly pursued to the boat, where he barely succeeded in making his escape.

Leland's captors took up their march toward the Ohio. Here, although their captive was suffering intense agony, they forced him into the water, and compelled him to swim across. Every stroke he thought would be his last, yet he reached the shore in safety. The band set forward at once. There were six savages, upon two of whom the duty of attending Leland devolved. Yet he required little watching or attention. The thought of escape was far from his mind ; he was in a sad situation to rebel or offer resistance. Both hands were firmly secured behind him, and his strength was taxed to the utmost to keep up with his captors.

In the course of a couple of hours they came upon two of their companions, seated around and amusing themselves with a negro. Each appeared to enjoy himself prodigiously at the expense of the poor African, who was boiling over with furious rage.

" Get out, niggers !" he shouted, " my head's split wide open now, sure !"

Here one of the savages amused himself by letting the end of a weighty stick fall upon the head of the negro. The luxuriant wool caused it to rebound again, to the infinite delight of the tormentors, who smiled horribly at it.

Leland recognized Zeb as he came up. It gave him a sort of pleasure, or rather served to lighten his pain, to know that they were to be companions in captivity. He could probably obtain information of Rosalind, while the conversation of the slave might assist to keep off the gloom which was settling over him.

"Gorra, ef dar ain't massa Leland," exclaimed the negro, turning toward the approaching Indians. "High! whar'd *you* come from, George? What did you let 'em cotch *you* fur?"

"Because I could not prevent it," returned he, with a faint smile.

"Well, now, if't had been dis pusson, you see, dey'd 've had some trouble."

"How is it that you are here, then?"

"Well, dat question requires considerable explanation. I know'd as how dey's agoin' to git *you*, and so I just come along to help you out de scrape."

Here the conversation ceased for the present. Leland had stretched himself upon the ground, and the pain of his wound increased. A savage noticing this, prepared a sort of poultice of pounded leaves and herbs, and placed it upon his side. Had this been done with a view to alleviate his suffering and not to preserve him for a great and awful torture, as it really was, Leland might have felt disposed to thank him for it.

It had now begun to grow dark. A fire was started, and in a short time a large quantity of meat was roasted. A piece of this was offered to Leland, but, though a short time before he had felt keenly the pangs of hunger, the sight of food now filled him with loathing.

"S'posen you offer dis pusson a few pounds, just to see if he'll take it," suggested Zeb, gazing wistfully toward the Indian who held it.

Several pieces were given him, all of which he devoured voraciously and demanded more. An Indian approached him, and holding a piece within a few inches of his mouth, jerked it away as he was about to seize it. This was repeated several times, until Zeb, losing all patience, became morose and

sullen and refused to snap at it. The savage seemed disposed
to humor him and held it still closer. Zeb, watching his
opportunity, made a quick motion, and nearly severed the
finger of his tormentor's hand, between his teeth. The savage
dropped the meat with a howl, and furiously shaking his
wounded member, fairly danced with pain. He would have
undoubtedly killed the negro had not his companions prevented. They enjoyed the sport and encouraged Zeb, who
devoured his food for some time in dignified silence.

"Wouldn't mind tryin' some more. S'poseu you hold out
yer other hand!"

No one noticed this remark, and the negro was obliged to
rest satisfied with what he had obtained.

As night came on, the savages stretched themselves upon
the earth and left the prisoners to themselves. Each was
securely fastened. Leland was within a few feet of Zeb, yet
he concluded to wait until all were asleep before he ventured
to hold converse with him.

At length, when the night had considerably advanced, and
the heavy breathing of the savages showed that slumber had
at last settled upon them, George turned his head so that he
faced the negro, and abruptly asked :

"Zeb, what do you know of my sister ?"

"Noffin' !" returned the negro, earnestly.

"Were you not taken off together?"

"At fust we was; but dey took her one way and me
anoder." He then proceeded to narrate all the circumstances
which had occurred to him, since the burning of the house,
in his own characteristic way.

"I am afraid you will soon have your last adventure," said
Leland.

"Gorra ! does you s'pose dat dey'd dare to shake a stick at
me when I's mad."

"I think they were engaged at that when I came up."

"Well, dat you see is a mistake."

"Have you heard any thing hinted of the manner in which
they intend to dispose of you ?"

"Not much, but I consates dat I knows. Dey'll just make
me dar chief, if I'll stay wid 'em, and I's bout 'cluded dat I
would, just so dat I can pay 'em for dis trick."

"Have they made the proposition yet?" asked George, feeling a strange impulse to amuse himself.

"Well, 'bout as good. Dey axed me not to hurt 'em, and said somefin' 'bout tying somebody to a tree and roastin' 'em. S'pose dey's 'fraid I'll do it to all ob em one dese days, if dey isn't careful."

"Why do they misuse you, if they intend to elevate you?"

"Well, dat's hard to tell. They've gone and went and cut all my curls off."

"Never mind such things," said Leland, again feeling depressed. "In all probability neither you nor I will see many more days. Unless we are rescued pretty soon, we shall be past all human help. I advise you, Zeb, to let serious thoughts enter your mind. Think of the world which you are soon to enter, and try and make some preparation for it."

The negro gazed wonderingly at Leland, then turned his head without speaking. The words probably had some effect upon him, for he made no further observations. His silence seemed occasioned by the doom pending over him.

That night was one never to be forgotten by Leland. The pain of his wound, and the still greater pain of his thoughts, prevented a moment's sleep. Hour after hour he gazed into the smoldering embers before him, buried in deep meditation, and conjuring up fantastic figures in the glowing coals. Then he watched the few stars which were twinkling through the branches overhead, and the sighing of the solemn night-wind made music that chorded with the feelings of his soul.

Far in the small hours of the night, he lay still awake sending up his prayer to the only eye that saw him, and to the only one that could assist him.

CHAPTER IX.

ZEB'S REVENGE.

WHEN the King of Terrors shakes his sword at his victim, unwonted yearnings come over the human heart. To die alone, removed from home and friends, when strange faces are beside us, is a fate which we all fervently pray may not be ours. Yet, when these strangers are enemies, and our death is at their hands—when every shriek or moan elicits only jeers and laughter, how unspeakably dreadful is the fate! He who has lost a dear friend in war, that has languished and died in the hands of strangers, and perhaps received no burial at their hands—he who mourns such a loss, may be able to appreciate, in some degree, the mournful situation of young Leland, in the hands of the malignant Shawnees.

It is at such times as these, if at no other, that the stricken and bowed heart turns to the One who alone can cheer and sustain. When shut out from all prospect of human help, and conscious that there is but one arm which is not shortened, we do not draw back from calling upon that arm to sustain us in the dark hour of trial.

With the dull glow of the slumbering camp-fire, the grotesque groups of almost unconscious sleepers, the solemn sighing of the night-wind, and the twinkle of the stars through the branches overhead—with such mournful surroundings as these, George Leland sent up his prayer of agony to God.

He prayed, not for life, but for the preparation to meet the death impending. The soft wailing of the night-zephyr seemed to warn him that the death-angel was approaching every moment. He prayed for his beloved sister in the hands of ruthless enemies—prayed only as he could pray when he realized her peril. And he sent up his petition for the safety of Leslie, who might still be awaiting his return—for the rough ranger with him, and for the rude, untutored negro, now his brother-prisoner.

A short distance away, he could discern the shadowy form of Zeb, bound against a tree, while scattered around him were stretched the savage sentinels, whether asleep or not he was unable to tell. As for that matter, however, they might as well have been unconscious as awake, for the slumber of the North American Indian is so delicate that a falling leaf is sufficient to disturb it.

The heart of Leland bled for the poor ignorant colored man. His prolonged silence showed that he had begun to realize, in some measure, his appalling situation. His natural thoughtlessness and recklessness could not last forever. It might carry him into many a danger, but not *beyond* it.

The Shawnees seemed to imagine that the bonds of the prisoners were secure, and that there was no possibility of their escape. In fact, Leland had no hopes of release. Had his hands been free, he might have ventured to do something; but at present they were as useless as if he were deprived altogether of those members.

It was fully an hour beyond midnight, when, in spite of his situation, Leland began to yield to the fatigue of the day. His head drooped upon his breast, and he started fitfully. It is at such times as these that the nervous system seems to be most fully alive to what is passing. The prisoner was just in this state of mind when his attention was arrested by a sound no louder than the murmuring wind above him—so low, indeed, that it would have escaped his attention altogether, had it not been of a character different from that monotonous moaning.

With the consciousness of this sound, came also the knowledge that it was a continuous one, and had been in progress some time. At first it seemed to be in the tree above him, but a moment's listening proved that it came from the direction of the negro, Zeb. The darkness had deepened somewhat during the last hour, so that he could barely make the outline of the fellow, but could not discern any motion upon his part, unless it was an absolute change of position.

All doubt as to Zeb being the author of the disturbing sound was removed as soon as Leland became fully awake. It came directly from toward him, and was of such a nature that it could not have been caused by one of the sleeping

Shawnees. With his eyes intently fixed upon the shadowy outlines of the negro, Leland saw the upper part of his body move forward, and then suddenly straighten itself again. This singular movement was repeated several times, and then, to his amazement, he saw the African step clear away from the tree and approach him!

As Zeb deposited his foot upon the ground, it was slowly and cautiously, and at each time he threw his outstretched arms upward, like a bird when flying, distorting his face also, as if the effort caused him extreme pain. But he passed the sleepers safely, and was soon beside his master.

"How did you succeed in freeing yourself?" he asked.

"Golly, I chawed 'em off!" he replied, with a suppressed chuckle. "Had a great notion of chawin' de tree off, sd dat it mought fall on dem and broke dar necks."

"'Sh! you are making too much noise," admonished Leland, in a guarded whisper.

"Shall I eat up your cords?"

"Loosen them around my wrists and arms, and then I will help myself."

"Yere's de instruments dat will do dat same t'ing," said Zeb, applying himself to the task at once. He progressed with such celerity and success that in a few moments, to Leland's unspeakable delight, he found his arms at liberty. It need scarcely be said that these were immediately used to assist the negro in his further efforts.

The excitement and nervousness of the young man were so great, that when his limbs were freed of the fetters he was scarcely able to stand, and, for a few moments, was on the very verge of fainting. The sudden renewal of hope overcame him for the time. By a powerful effort he regained his self-possession, and strove, in the few hurried seconds that were his, to decide upon some means of action.

It may be said that the two prisoners were literally surrounded by savages. They were stretched on every side of them, and before either dare hope to escape, it was necessary (if the expression be allowable) to scale the dreaded prison-wall. Leland had good cause to fear success for himself and his sable companion in this attempt. He found, to his chagrin and dismay, that scarcely any reliance at all could be placed upon his own limbs. His legs especially, from their long confinement in one position, were so cramped and spasmodic, that, when he stepped out from the tree to join the negro, one of them doubled like a reed beneath him and let him fall to the ground. He believed it was all over with him; but his fall was so gentle as not to disturb the sleepers, and he once more raised himself to his feet.

"Shan't I carry dat sick leg while you walk wid de oder one?" inquired Zeb, in a sympathetic tone.

"It is almost useless to me at present," replied Leland. "Let me lean upon you while we walk, and for the love of heaven, Zeb, be cautious. A single mismove, and it will be all up with us."

"Strikes dis chile dat it was ober wid you jes' now, de way you cawalloped onto de ground jes' now."

"My leg is asleep and numb."

"Let's wake it up, den."

Leland paused a few moments until the circulation was somewhat restored; but, as every moment seemed so fraught with peril to him, he whispered to the negro to move ahead, repeating his petition for him to exercise the most extreme caution in all his movements.

After all, the young man knew that the peril of both lay in the habitual recklessness of the ignorant fellow.

At first Zeb entirely overdid the matter. The trained elephant that steps over the prostrate and pompous form of Van Amburgh, was not more careful and tardy in the performance of his feat than was the negro in passing the unconscious form of a Shawnee. Although Leland deemed this circumspection unnecessary, he did not protest, as he feared, in case he did so, the negro would run into the opposite extreme.

The foot of Zeb was lifted in the very act of stepping over the third and last savage, when a smoldering ember parted, and a twist of flame flared up. At that instant, he looked down and recognized in the features of the Indian, the one who had taken such especial delight in tormenting him through the day. The negro paused while he was yet astride of him.

"Look dar!" he whispered, "dat's him; tired himself out

so much pullin' at my wool, dat he is sleepin' like a chicken in de egg."

Leland made no reply, but motioned for him to proceed; but Zeb stubbornly maintained his position.

"Look what a mouf he has!" he added; "tremenjus! If 'twas only two, free inches wider on each side, he mought outshine me; but it's no use de way de affair is got up jes' now."

"Go on! go on!" repeated Leland, shoving him impatiently with his hand.

"In jes' one minit. Dat's him dat bothered me so much to-day. I'd like to smoke him for it! Gorra! if he hain't woke. Dar—take dat!"

The savage, who had been awakened and alarmed by the voice of the negro, received a smashing blow in his face, that straightened him out completely. Realizing his imminent peril, Leland at once leaped away in the woods at the top of his speed, the negro taking a direction almost opposite. Every Shawnee was aroused; the critical moment for the fugitives was upon them.

CHAPTER X.

THE BRIEF REPRIEVE.

LELAND succeeded in getting outside the circle of savages when, feeling himself in the open woods, he dashed away a the top of his speed. He ran with astonishing swiftness f a few moments, when, as might naturally be expected, he e exhausted himself that he was scarcely able to stand.

From the moment of starting, the Shawnees seemed to understand the identity of the fugitives; and while they did not neglect to send in pursuit of the flying negro, four of their fleetest runners instantly dashed after the white man. Were it in the daylight, the latter would not have stood a moment's chance against them; but he hoped to elude them in the darkness and gloom of the woods. The obscuration being only partial, his pursuers close in his rear, and the noise of the rustling leaves beneath his feet betraying every step, it will be seen at once that he was in the most constant and imminent danger.

Pausing but a few seconds—barely sufficient to catch his "second breath," he again leaped away. There is no telling how long he would have run, had he not stepped into a hole, deep and narrow—the mouth of a fox's burrow evidently, for it was quite hidden by overgrowth—he fell into the hole with a sudden violence which confused and stunned him. Panting and exhausted, he lay still and awaited his pursuers.

They were far closer than he imagined. He seemed scarcely to have disappeared, when the whole four passed within a few feet of him. How fearfully his heart throbbed as the foot of one threw several leaves upon his person !

Leland had lain here less than five minutes, when a second footstep startled him. It came from an entirely different direction ; and approaching to within about a dozen feet, it halted. Rising to his hands and feet so that his head was brought upon a level with the ground, he peered through the darkness at the object. One long, earnest, scrutinizing look, revealed the dress of a large Indian. His position was so favorable that he could even make out the rifle he held in his hand.

He stood as motionless as a statue for a moment, and then gave utterance to a cry that resembled exactly that of the whippowil. Receiving no response, he repeated it again, but with no better success than before. The cowering fugitive was listening for the slightest movement upon his part, when to his unfeigned amazement, the Indian in a suppressed whisper called out, " *Leland !*"

The young man, however, was not thrown off his guard. He knew that every one of his captors spoke the English language, some of them quite fluently. It need scarcely be said that he made no response to the call, even when it was iterated again and again. The savage during these utterances did not stir a hand or foot, but seemed to bend all his faculties into the one of listening. He had stood but a few moments, when Leland caught the rustle of approaching feet.

The Indian detected them at the same moment, and instantly moved off, but with such a catlike tread that the young man scarcely heard him at all. Ah! had he but known the identity of that strange Indian, and responded to his call, he would have been saved!

It was scarcely a moment later when the whole four Indians came back at a leisurely gait, and halted not more than a rod from where Leland imagined he lay concealed. They commenced conversing at once in broken English:

"White man got legs of deer—run fast," said one.

"Yeh!—git away from four Shummumdewumrum—run much fast," added another.

"Go back to camp—stay dere—won't come among Shawnee ag'in—don't like him, t'ink."

"He run much fast—mebbe fast as black man."

At this point the whole four laughed immoderately, as if in remembrance of the ludicrous figure of Zeb. Their mirth continued for several moments, when they sobered down and renewed their conversation.

"Wait till daylight—den foller trail t'rough woods—Shummumdewumrum git eye on it—soon cotch him."

This Leland felt was now his great danger. Should his pursuers return to their camp, he hoped the distance that he thus gained upon them would be sufficient to carry him entirely beyond their reach; but if they decided to remain where they were, his only chance was to steal away before the morning came. Judging such to be their intention, he determined to make the attempt at once.

On his hands and knees he commenced crawling forward, listening to every word that was uttered.

"White man try hard to git away—don't like Shawnee great much."

"He run much fast, *den fall down in woods !*"

"*Den try to crawl away like snake !*"

Leland saw that it was all over with him and gave up at once. The Indians had been aware of his hiding-place from the moment he fell, and their passage beyond it, their return and their conversation, were all made on purpose to toy with his fears, as a cat would play with a mouse before destroying it.

As one of the savages uttered the last words, he walked directly to the prostrate man, and ordered him to arise. Leland judged it best to resist no further. He accordingly obeyed; and, saddened and despairing, was led back a prisoner to the Indian camp.

We have heard of a fish, known in the humble fisherman's parlance as the *ink-fish*, which, when pursued by an enemy, has the power of tinging the water in its immediate vicinity with such a dark color, that its pursuer is completely befogged and gives up the hopeless chase in disgust.

A realizing sense of his recklessness and his imminent peril came over Zeb when he felled the rising Shawnee to the earth. It was his intention, in the first place, to serve every one in the same manner; but as they came to their feet far more rapidly than he anticipated, he gave over the idea, and, with a "Ki! yi!" plunged headlong into the woods. At this very juncture, the attention of the Indians was taken up with Leland, as the more important captive of the two, and for a moment the negro escaped notice; but the instant the four started after him, two others gave Zeb their undivided attention.

The sable fugitive, with all his recklessness, did the very best thing that could have been done under the circumstances. Instead of fleeing, as did Leland, he ran less than a hundred yards, when he halted abruptly and took a position behind a sapling. Here he stood as motionless as death, while his enemies came on. Whether his intensely black countenance had the power of diffusing deeper darkness into the surrounding gloom, or whether it was the unexpected manner of his flight that deluded his pursuers, we are unable to say. Certain it is that although the two savages passed very closely to him, neither saw nor suspected his presence.

"Gorra, but dat's soothin'," chuckled Zeb. "Dey've missed me dis time, shuah! Wonder whether dey'll outlive dar disapp'intment, when dey finds out dat when dey finds me, dey hain't found me! Ki! yi!"

He maintained his motionless position for several moments longer, all the while listening for his enemies. As their footsteps finally died out in the distance, and he realized that he was left alone indeed, his former characteristic returned to him.

"What's to be done, dat *am* de question !" said he, speaking in an incautiously loud voice, as he spread out his left hand at the same time, and rested the forefinger of his right upon it. "In de *fust* place, I don't know what has become of Master Leland. If he's done got away, how am I to find him ? If I sets up a yell to cotch his ear, like 'nuff de oders will hear it also likewise. Den if he hasn't got away what *am* de use ob bawlin' to him. Guess I won't bawl."

So much was settled at least. The fact that it would not only be a useless but an extremely dangerous undertaking to make an outcry at that particular time, worked itself through his head, and the intention was accordingly given over for the present.

"One thing *am* sartin, howsumever," he added. "I'm hungry, and I know dar am some meat left by dat camp-fire, dat would relish high jus' now. But had I oughter to go dar or not ? Dey mought found me, but den I'm hungry."

When our own personal feelings are put into the balance, they are apt to outweigh the dictates of prudence and sense. The experiences of the night, although fraught in their teachings to the ignorant black man, had not as yet attained sufficient dignity to stand before the animal feelings of his nature.

Although he comprehended in a degree the risk he run, he decided it was worth his while to do it, rather than suffer for a few hours longer the cravings of what was only a moderate degree of hunger.

"De stummich am de most importantest part ob man, and consequently am de fust thing dat should receive his undi‧wided attention."

With this philosophical conclusion, he turned his footsteps toward the camp-fire. Despite its proximity, he experienced considerable difficulty in finding it. The few smoldering embers, gleaming like a demon's eye, guided him, however, to the spot.

"Dar *am* anoder matter sartin," thought he, as he came up. "Mr. Zebenezer Langdon is not agwine to be able to s'arch here br de meat onless he has some more light—Ki ! dat coal am warm!" he exclaimed, as he hopped off from the fiery end of a fagot.

It required but a few moments to gather sufficient fuel to replenish the fire. The hot coals set the wood almost immediately into a roaring blaze, which threw a warm, rich light through the surrounding woods for many yards around.

Zeb was radiant with smiles. The cool night and the constrained position had chilled him considerably, and he gave the fire a few moments to infuse the comfortable warmth into his person.

"Now I'll jes' warm up my hands like," said he, after a few minutes, "and den I'll go to work;" and forthwith he held them toward the blaze, rubbing and turning them into each other with great zest and enjoyment.

"*Dar*, I guess dat'll do. Now I'll make a s'arch—Gorra! whar did *you* come from?"

As the negro turned, he found himself standing face to face with the two Shawnees who had started in his pursuit but a short time before! He realized that he was recaptured, and made no resistance. He was instantly re-bound to the very tree from which he had escaped, while the Indians sat upon the ground very near him, firmly resolved that he should not again have so favorable an opportunity to leave them.

The negro was hardly secured, when the other savages made their appearance with Leland. He was also fastened to the identical tree from which he had been loosened: and there, sad, gloomy and despairing, he was left until morning.

CHAPTER XI.

A FRIEND.

In a short time the whole body of Indians were awake and astir. The morning meal was soon prepared and hastily eaten, and they set forward. Leland found that his wound was much better, and he traveled without difficulty. The savages took a southerly direction, and appeared to be journeying toward the destination of those who held Rosalind.

Their march continued without interruption until noon, when they halted for a couple of hours for rest and food. For the first time, George partook of some, and felt in a more hopeful frame of mind. Zeb was as usual, and continued quarreling with and abusing and threatening every one within his reach.

"If dis isn't shameful, treating a pusson like me in dis way. I's sorry dat I ever come wid you. I 'spects ebery bone in my body is broke in pieces."

"You said last night that they dare not touch you," interrupted Leland.

"Well, dat's a subject dat you can't understand, and I haven't time to 'splain it. Dey're perwoken, anyhow, and dey's agwine to cotch dar pay some ob dese days."

Consoled with this reflection, Zeb kept steadily upon his way, seemingly as happy as a person could be when laboring under a slight provocation. No further words passed between him and Leland for a considerable time. The latter was busy with his own thoughts, and began to feel the fatigues of their long-continued journey. They had set out at an early hour, and had halted only at noon. The traveling was very difficult at times, often leading through tangled underwood and swamps, where a person's weight bore him deep into the mire; and now and then some sluggish, poisonous serpent crawled from beneath their feet, or hissed at them from some decayed tree.

About the middle of the afternoon they paused upon the

banks of a stream of considerable size, which was a tributary to the Big Sandy. Though broad, it was not deep, and could be easily forded. The water flowed quite swiftly, and being perfectly translucent, the bottom could be seen from either shore.

Here the Indians exhibited their usual cunning and foresight. During their journey, they had proceeded in "Indian file," permitting their prisoners, however, to walk after their usual manner. The reason for their adopting the caution mentioned with themselves, was more from habit than any thing else. Although suspecting they might be pursued, yet they had little fear of an enemy, and omitted, as we have seen, to employ a sentinel at night.

One of the savages stepped into the water, and, taking a few steps, was followed by another, who placed his feet upon the stones, in the tracks that he had used and made. Thus each one did until Leland and Zeb were driven in and warned to do likewise. The former had no difficulty in obeying, but the latter, either through mistake or design, made several provoking blunders. He seemed to use his utmost endeavors to step into the tracks of those before him, but instead of succeeding, was sure to place his foot a good distance from it; and losing his foothold when about in the center of the stream, came down with an awkward splash into the water.

"Gorra!" he exclaimed, regaining his position, "dat fish pulled awful." The savages nearest cast threatening looks toward him, and he reached the shore without further mishap.

At about sundown the party came to a halt, and a fire was started. Leland and Zeb found themselves in the same condition as upon the preceding night, with the exception that a closer surveillance was kept upon their actions. George partook sparingly of supper, while Zeb's appetite was as insatiate as ever. A guard was stationed as soon as it was fully dark, and the Indians appeared disposed to amuse and enjoy themselves until a late hour. One of their number, with a hoarse, guttural "Ugh!" approached the negro.

"You needn't come here," ejaculated Zeb, divining his intention. The savage paid no attention to him, but continued approaching. Had the negro been free, he might have offered resistance and occasioned considerable trouble; but besides haviug his arms bound, his legs were joined at the ankles and he was thus rendered helpless.

"Plenty wool," said the savage, placing his hand upon his head. He made no answer, but glanced furtively and suspiciously at him. "Nice, good," he added; then closing his hand, gave a vigorous jerk.

"Lord help me!" screamed Zeb, rolling over in helpless agony.

"Poor fellow," repeated the Indian, approaching him and rubbing his back, after the manner which a celebrated horse-tamer advises. Then, watching his opportunity, he seized another quantity and pulled it forth. To his surprise, this elicited no remark from his victim, and he repeated it.

This time he succeeded no better than before.

Zeb was lying upon his back and staring at his tormentor in unspeakable fury. The Indian, still determined upon amusement, again approached. Zeb remained motionless until he stooped over him; then bending his knees to his chin, he gathered all his strength, and planted both feet in his chest, throwing him a dozen feet. The savage groaned and doubled up in his agony, and gasped spasmodically for breath.

"Dar, how does *dat* set on your stummich? Yah! yah! dat's fun!"

Although this for the moment amused the others, yet it likewise excited their anger, and there is no telling what the end would have been, had not their attention been suddenly called in another direction. This was occasioned by the arrival of a stranger among them.

Leland gazed at the new-comer, and saw a tall, powerfully-built and well-shaped savage stalk boldly forward toward the fire, and exchange salutations with those seated around. All regarded him suspiciously at first, yet his boldness and assurance seemed to disarm them, and room was made for him. The pipe was passed to him, and taking it, he smoked several minutes in silence, during which time he seemed unconscious that the eye of every one was bent upon him. Having finished, he turned and passed it to the one nearest him, then gazing thoughtfully for a few moments in the fire, commenced a conversation with the chief. He spoke their tongue as correctly and fluently as any of them, which served to disarm them still more. He stated that he had been out with a couple of Indians, scouring the country for prey, when they were set upon and pursued by two hunters, who at the first shot killed his companion. He succeeded in effecting his escape after a hot pursuit of nearly a day, and encountering a trail which he supposed to be his friends', he followed it up and found that he was not mistaken.

On hearing this recital, several of the savages appeared to suspect that Kent and Leland were the two to whom he referred, and directed his attention toward their captives. The savage stared wonderingly toward them for a moment, and slowly shook his head. He had never seen either before.

Although none of the Indians could show any reason for suspecting their visitor, except his strange arrival among them, still they were not reckless and foolish enough to leave him to himself, or to permit him to depart. Besides the two who were stationed at a distance as sentinels, one remained awake to keep an eye upon his movements. Yet this precaution was useless; for to all appearances, he slept as deeply as any of them, and was among the latest who awoke in the morning.

Leland fell asleep about midnight, and gained a few hours of undisturbed rest. In the morning he was considerably refreshed, and had it not been for the awful doom that threatened him, would have possessed a joyous fund of spirits. His wound, which had been only an ugly flesh one, had ceased to trouble him, and he experienced no pain except from the ligaments that bound him. As he increased in strength, these were increased in number and tightness, until his limbs swelled and pained him more than his hurt.

It is the same with the body as with the mind. The sorest affliction that can visit us will not occasion half the murmuring and discontent that the petty annoyances and grievances of every-day life. Could the pain which harassed Leland, and in the end nearly drove him frantic, have been concentrated into a few moments, or even into a half-hour, he could have borne it without a murmur; but it was the continual, never-ceasing, monotonous length of it that troubled him.

Several times in the course of their journey, Leland was upon the point of beseeching his enemies to kill him at once, and end his misery; and had he reason to believe that they would have gratified him, he would not have hesitated a moment; but such a request would have been useless.

At noon, as usual, the party came to a halt, and a couple proceeded to bind Leland to a tree. During the proceeding he broke the cords that pained him so much, and they were replaced by others. The latter, however, were much more lax, and he felt greatly relieved when they were placed upon him.

As soon as he was secured to the body of the tree, the savage left him and joined his companions. Leland closed his eyes as if to shut out the terrible reality, and the dancing lights that flickered before him, together with the hum that filled his ears, told him that for a moment he had succeeded. But he was soon recalled to a sense of his situation by the *zip* of a tomahawk within a few inches of his head. Opening his eyes, he soon comprehended the state of things. The savages were amusing themselves by ascertaining who could send his tomahawk nearest the body of their captive without touching him. The first weapon that had been sent had missed his head, as we have said, by a few inches; but the next was still closer, and Leland felt the wind of it, as it buried itself in the solid oak by his cheek. He again closed his eyes, and fervently prayed that one of their hatchets might sink into his skull instead of the tree; yet there was not much danger of such an occurrence; for the savages exercised perfect skill, and rarely failed of sending their weapons to the very point intended.

Leland opened his eyes as a tomahawk came fearfully close to his forehead. He wished to see who had hurled it. He soon saw that it was the strange Indian, who was approaching to withdraw it. It was buried deeper than the others; and as the savage placed his hand upon it, it required considerable of an effort to extricate it. While doing so, Leland heard the following words whispered by the stranger:

"Don't be scart, George; it's Kent Whiteman that has got his eye upon you."

These words came near proving fatal to both. They so startled Leland that he could not prevent himself from betraying somewhat his emotion and excitement. This was observed by a savage near at hand, who approached to satisfy himself of the cause. Leland, suspecting his motive, repeated the action and accompanied it by a shudder, as though the scene which was being enacted had overcome him. This satisfied the wily Indian, who retreated and joined the others.

Hope was again awakened in Leland's breast—painful hope, that increased his doubts and fears—hope that drowned the torture that beset him—hope that sent the life-blood coursing rapidly and hotly through his veins, and increased the charms which life had held out to him.

Leland was shortly released from his unenviable situation, and Zeb put in his place. The negro made no threats or declaration, but submitted to the trying ordeal without a word. The scenes through which he had passed had evidently had some effect upon him. He seemed to possess a faint realization of the danger in which he and his companion were placed. And yet it could not be said that he was really frightened, for he evinced no fear of any of his enemies, and his silence had the appearance of being occasioned by sullenness and apathy. He did not tremble in the least, but gazed unflinchingly at the tomahawks, as they came revolving and seemingly directed toward his head, and struck beside him.

Finding that they had about lost their power over their captives, the Indians released Zeb, and permitted him and his master to lie down upon the ground.

Leland could not prevent his gaze from wandering toward Kent now and then, yet their eyes did not meet. The latter betrayed no interest whatever in either of the captives, and seemed as indifferent to their fate as any of the others.

The negro had no suspicion of the true state of things, and perhaps it was the best that he had not. He might have unwittingly betrayed it, and Kent did not choose to warn him. The fact was, it could have done him but little good at any rate; for Kent had determined to rescue Leland, if possible, and leave Zeb for the present to shift for himself. The white man was the first upon whom they would wreak their vengeance, and aside from the greater estimation in which his life was held, from the very nature of the case, he required the first attention.

CHAPTER XII.

ESCAPE.

THE hunter in the course of the day had gained a full knowledge of the intentions of the Indians in regard to their captives. Leland was to suffer death at the stake at an early period, while the negro was to be reserved until some indefinite time in the future, to be tortured.

The hunter had completely succeeded in disarming his enemies of every suspicion. He had employed himself, as we have seen, in throwing his tomahawk at Leland; and learning through a casual remark that he was to be put to the torture, he expressed his opinion strongly in favor of it, urging them at the same time to do it as soon as possible. He made himself perfectly at home, and was so free among them, that a stranger would have considered him one of the leading characters.

So perfectly had Kent dissembled, that at night, unexpectedly to himself, he was chosen as one to watch Leland. The negro was firmly fastened to a tree and left to himself, while George was to sleep between two savages.

At supper-time Kent brought him a good-sized piece of well-cooked meat, and gave him to understand that he was to eat it at all events. Leland took it without daring to meet his benefactor's eye, and ate all that was possible. The negro received his meal from the same hand without the remotest suspicion that a friend was so near him, and even went so far as to insult him as much as was in his power, for not bringing him a larger quantity of food. To carry out still further the appearance of things, Kent tore a small tuft from the negro's head, as if to revenge himself.

"Blast you," he shouted, "if I doesn't flog you till you can't stand. Just hold out your paw a minute."

Zeb used his utmost powers of persuasion to induce Kent to reach his hand toward him, hoping to revenge himself as he had upon a former occasion; but the hunter was too shrewd for him, and with a threatening gesture, left him to himself, and joined his companions.

"Gorra!" said Zeb to Leland, "if I doesn't believe dat dat's de nigger I sawed up in de barn toder day."

"You mean cut up?"

"'All de same; leastways ef 'tis him, he's cotched his pay afore he come sneakin' about here."

Now that Leland knew assistance was at hand, he experienced a desire to converse with the negro, and thus help to pass away time, which had grown intolerably monotonous. Turning to the old slave, he resumed :

"He is a savage-looking individual."

This was said in order to quell any suspicion or doubt that might have entered his head.

"Dat he is; but he'd better keep away from me, if he doesn't want his picter sp'iled," returned the negro.

"What were you abusing him for, a few minutes ago, when he brought your food?"

"Well, you see, he's afraid I's agwine to hurt him, and begun to beg off. It makes me *so* mad to see any feller afraid dat I let out on him, and he took himself off in a mighty big hurry."

"Have you lost much of your wool?"

"Two or free hands full; dat's all. 'Bout all growed in ag'in; but I ca'culate dat de next dat gits his hand in my head 'll get it in a steel-trap. If I gits my grinder on 'im he'll see," said Zeb, with a meaning shake of his head.

"I guess that they will not trouble you further for the present," added Leland, with that air of assurance which one feels for the safety of another when his own case is free from danger.

"Don't know 'bout dat, but I'd like to have 'em try."

"Well, your wish is about to be gratified," said Leland, as he noticed a savage approaching him.

"Gorra, don't come here!" said Zeb, staring at him. The savage did not heed his warning, however, but continued to advance, and made a motion as if to strike him. The black man closed his eyes, bent his head toward him and drew his face in all manner of furious contortions. The savage, however, left him without provoking him further.

Leland was allowed to remain in his position until the savages stretched themselves out to rest. They remained up later than usual, smoking and recounting their deeds and boasting of the exploits they intended to accomplish. Kent narrated some marvelous stories, which greatly excited their wonder and admiration of him.

The time thus occupied seemed interminable to Leland, who was in a fever of excitement and anxiety; but at last Kent stretched himself beside him, while the other watch did the same upon the opposite side.

Still it would probably be hours before any thing could be done, and Leland was compelled to suffer the most intense and anxious impatience for a long time. His thoughts prevented him from feeling the least desire to sleep, and he could only worry and writhe in his helpless position.

Kent, in arranging a place for himself beside him, bent his head to his ear and breathed:

"Pretend to sleep."

Although this was said in less than a whisper, Leland heard the words distinctly and prepared to follow the warning. To prevent the slightest suspicion, he continued to groan and move for some minutes; but he gradually ceased, and after a while settled down into a state of rest. Soon his heavy, regular breathing would have led any one into the belief that a heavy sleep was upon him. Not the slightest voluntary motion was made, and Kent remarked to his brother sentinel that their captive must be unconscious of the doom that awaited him.

A cord was fastened to Leland's wrist and then to Kent's arm, so that the slightest movement upon the part of the former would disturb and awake the latter should he fall asleep. The other watch, noticing this, failed to adopt the same precaution.

For a few more minutes the savage held a conversation with Kent; but in the course of a half-hour the answers of the latter began to grow brief and indistinct, and finally ceased altogether; then he began to breathe more slowly and heavily, and the savage at last believed that both guard and prisoner were sound asleep.

When lying upon the earth at night, with no one with whom a conversation can be held, and with nothing but the will to combat the approach of sleep, the person is almost sure to succumb sooner or later. At any rate, such was the case with the savage in question, and scarce an hour had elapsed since he had ceased speaking when he was as unconscious of the state of things around as though he had never been born.

Now was the time to commence operations; the critical moment had arrived, and Kent commenced the work upon which probably more than one life depended.

First he withdrew his knife from his belt, and severed the cord that bound him to Leland. Then as cautiously, silently and quickly, cut the thong that held his feet. This was the first intimation Leland had that his friend was at work.

Leland's hands, as we have said, were bound behind; consequently it was necessary that he should turn upon his side in order that Kent might reach them. He knew this and made the movement; but his excitement and agitation were so great that he turned too far, and in recovering himself, awoke the savage. His presence of mind and Kent's cunning saved him. He groaned deeply and muttered to himself, while the hunter started up as though he had just awoke, and gazed wonderingly at him.

"I wish he'd keep still," said he, in the Indian tongue, lying down again. This satisfied the other, who fell back and closed his eyes.

For an hour neither stirred. At the end of that time, Kent raised his head and gazed cautiously around upon the circle of sleeping savages. Zeb was at a short distance, resting as calmly as an infant upon its mother's breast. The one beside Leland had again passed off to the land of dreams; yet an Indian never sleeps soundly, and the slightest mishap upon the part of those who were awake and expecting to move, might arouse the whole body and bring certain and instant death upon them. It would not do to awaken the sleeping sentinel again. Life now hung upon a thread.

Kent reached beneath Leland and cut the cord. He was now free and at liberty to move.

"Be careful!" whispered the hunter, as he assisted him to his feet. Leland could not suppress his agitation, yet he used all the caution in his power. But cautious as they both were, the savage nearest them awoke. Kent had his eye upon him, and the instant he stirred, sprung like a panther toward him. One hand clutched his mouth, his knee pressed heavily upon his breast, and whipping out his knife, he forced it to the hilt in his body. Nothing but the dull, fleshy sound, as it sunk into the seat of life, was heard. The bloody stream silently followed its withdrawal, there were several spasmodic struggles, and the savage straightened out in death.

Kent arose from the body and motioned to Leland to follow him. Not another being was awake, and tremblingly he followed over their prostrate, sleeping forms. They were just passing into the thick surrounding darkness, when the negro, through some means, awoke.

"Gorra," he shouted, "isn't you gwine to help dis pusson too?"

"Cuss that nigger," muttered the hunter. "Keep close to me and use your pegs, fur a long run's before us."

Both darted away together, as the wild yells told them that their escape was discovered. Those horrid, unearthly whoops, of which no idea can be had unless they be heard, set Leland's blood on fire. In a moment the whole forest seemed swarming with their enemies, and the yells of many were fearfully near. Kent could distance any of them when alone, yet the presence of Leland retarded him somewhat. However, by taking the latter's hand, they both passed over the ground with great swiftness, and neither had much fear of being overtaken.

On, on plunged the pursued, until many a mile had been passed; still they halted not. The voices and answering shouts of the savages could be heard upon every side, and they had yet by no means reached a place of safety. Now some limb brushed in Leland's face, or he stumbled over some fallen tree, and then, without a murmur, arose and pursued his way. On, on they hurried, until the dispersing darkness told them that the day was not far distant.

"I can travel no further," said Leland, sinking to the earth.

"Give out?" queried Kent.

"I believe I have. This is a terrible chase; but the prospect of a recapture and death can not goad me further, until I have rested."

"Wal, no mistake we have tramped some; but Lord save you, this is just fun for me."

"Do you not think that they will abandon pursuit?"

"No danger of that. As soon as 'tis light they'll pounce upon our trail, and foller it until it's lost or we are cotched."

"Which must not be."

"Wal, p'raps if they get their claws on you you wouldn't feel very comfortable."

But they had passed through the most trying ordeals, and had now only to make their way as best they could. Kent had some idea of the nature of the ground, and they progressed with greater ease and rapidity, after a short rest.

"Here we are," said the hunter, coming to a halt. Leland gazed ahead, and saw a broad sheet of water which he knew must be the Ohio.

"And now," added Kent, "we've got to hunt up Leslie. He can't be far off, and I'm in hopes we'll stumble upon him afore day. Just squat and make yourself miserable while I take a run up and down the bank."

Leland obeyed him, and in a moment was left alone, shivering in the chilly night-air, and feeling miserable indeed in his lonely situation. But he was not disposed to murmur; he had escaped death—that was enough.

In the course of an hour Kent returned with the information that he had found the boat about half a mile up, but that Leslie was not in it. Both started, and, after stumbling over rushes loaded with water, and sinking into the miry shore, and wading in the river by turns, they came upon it, pulled igh up on the bank. It was becoming lighter every moment, and as Kent knew that as soon as possible their trail would be followed, he was unwilling to brook the slightest delay.

"As soon as one is out the scrape another gets in. Here you have got clear, and now *he* must go and make a fool of himself. If he's got taken, that's the meanest trick yet."

"Perhaps he is not far off," said Leland, stepping in the boat and searching it. "He is not here, certainly," he added, after looking over it.

"I'll wait awhile, and then we must look out for ourselves. No use of losing our own hair in tryin' to help him," rejoined Kent.

Both took the boat, and turning it over so as to free it from water, shoved it out from the beach.

Hallou, Leslie! If you're about just say so, and if you ain't, let us know," shouted Kent, in a loud voice.

A silence of a few moments followed, when he repeated the call. To the surprise of both it was answered.

"That you, Kent?" came a voice as if its owner had just waked.

"Wal, I rather guess so; and it's my private opinion that you'd better tumble yourself in here in short order," returned Kent.

A dark form arose to all appearance from the ground, and pitching awkwardly forward, exclaimed

"You don't suppose a fellow would be in the boat through all that rain, do you? Oh! is Leland there?" he asked, pausing and collecting his senses.

"No! Poor fellow's scalped and burned at the stake. Had to kill nine of them to save my own hair."

Leslie made no reply, but stepped silently into the boat. Making his way toward the stern, he encountered the very person of whom he had been speaking.

"Hey! who is this?" he exclaimed, starting back.

"A dead red-skin that I cotched," answered Kent.

"Leland, sure as I live!" said Leslie, joyously catching his hand.

For a few moments they heeded not the mirth of Kent at his joke, in their mutual congratulations. Then they turned and heard him say:

"What a couple of fools."

They appreciated his rough kindness too well to make any reply. The boat was out in the river, and under the long, powerful impulses that the hunter gave it, was moving rapidly downward.

CHAPTER XIII

THE CAPTIVE.

LELAND and Leslie conversed and recounted to each other their adventures until those were exhausted, when they endeavored to keep off the chill by taking turns at the oars. Morning at length began to appear. In a short time darkness lifted from the water, and the bright rays of the morning sun pierced the foliage of the forest and rested upon the stream.

About the middle of the forenoon, Kent ran in under the bank and sprung ashore. The day was quite warm, and it was a pleasure for the three to step upon the land and stretch themselves in the genial sunshine. They had, however, halted for consultation, and to determine upon the plan to pursue in order to rescue Rosalind.

"One more job finished and we'll rest awhile," said Kent.

"And as we have depended upon and been guided and saved by your wisdom," said Leslie, "of course, in this most important case your advice must be followed."

"Let's hear what you chaps have got to say first, 'cause p'raps you might accidentally say somethin' smart without knowin' it. I'll decide it after we all get through."

"What seems to me the most feasible is this," commenced Leland. "Let all three of us follow the savages which have taken my sister, and after reaching their vicinity, by stratagem recover her. If it be impossible to do it in this way, make a bold dash and venture among them, and take her at all events."

"Killin' first 'bout one hundred Injins, just to get 'em out the way, you know," said Kent, with mock gravity. "Come, Leslie, it's your turn; and bein' you're so much interested, I 'spects to hear somethin' awful grand."

Leslie, to save his life, could not prevent a blush at this allusion. As might be expected, he had thought of more than one plan, long before asked for it, and replied without hesitation:

"What I say is, *rescue* her at all events, as George has said. Of course, it's out of the question to do it by force, and we must outwit the savages. This I think possible, for the good reason that it has so often been done. All three of us, or perhaps, what would be better, you and myself can follow them up and retake her. George, in his present state, could do but little to aid us, and in all probability, will endanger the safety of all concerned."

" I agrees with you there ; and a little further. Mr. Leslie, in his present state,' *would* do but little to aid us, and in all probability, endanger the safety of all concerned."

"There is no need of jesting, Kent. You know that it would be the best for you to have a companion, and who can you take but me ?"

"Don't know but what it would. Now, s'posen an old feller that don't know nothin' says somethin' ?" said Kent, good-humoredly ; for he, as is generally the case with those of his class, had a habit of depreciating his own sagacity and foresight, when he really knew how much superior it was to his companion's.

"Don't know but what it would," he repeated. "S'pose if I's in your case, I'd feel the same ; but you see, there's somethin' else to think of. S'posen we gets her, we hain't got any place to stick our heads in, and may be hunted forever after by the skunks. Now as soon as convenient, we'll pad- dle down to the place where Leland's house was burned, and drop him there ; fur it won't do to take *you* 'long, George. Leslie understands the Injins better than you, and it would just git us all into a muss, and like enough, make 'em knock her on the head, to save trouble. We'll take you up to your farm 'cause that'll be a place we can't miss very well ; and if there's a shed or any thing left, you can stow yourself away till we gets back. Keep a good look-out, and don't get into any trouble. I'll take Leslie along, for I s'pose he won't stay, and I've thought of a plan that'll take him to work with. There, you have my plan."

" Which you must admit, is the one that must be followed," said Leslie, turning toward Leland.

"I suppose," he returned, "that your advice should be taken, although I confess that I had hoped to accompany you ; but as I said, Kent knows best, and the only proper course is to obey him."

"Well, let us not wait, now that we have decided what to
do," said Leslie, rising to his feet

"No; we ought to be movin', fur I opine we've a good
kamp afore us."

Again the boat was shoved out, and shot onward. Nothing
worthy of mention occurred on the way. The next day, at
noon, they reached their destination. Leland's heart sunk
within him, as he gazed up from the river and saw, where
once his home had been, nothing but black and charred ruins.
A portion of what had once been used as the barn remained
entire, having escaped the flames.

"This is just the thing," said Kent, approaching it. "We'll
fix it up a little and I'd advise you to go to sleep, and stay so
until we get back."

The three set vigorously to work, and in a short time they
had made it quite comfortable. It consisted of logs placed
firmly and compactly together, and secured so that a single
person well armed could offer effectual resistance to a formidable enemy. Being in a sort of clearing, it had the additional
advantage of affording its inhabitant such a view that he could
not be approached by any person without their being observed
and thus giving him time to prepare for them.

"There!" said the hunter, retreating a short distance and
gazing at it. "I wouldn't ax a better place. You might
bring down a hundred Injins, and give me plenty powder and
ball, I'd have the best fun in creation."

"Suppose they come upon all sides?" suggested Leland.

"All you got to do is to take the stock off your gun and
shoot out of both ends of the barrel."

"You can go now as soon as you please; but first tell me
what time to expect you back."

Kent folded both arms over the muzzle of his gun, and
shutting one eye, remained for a few moments buried in earnest thought. Then he replied:

"Between five and eight days; probably on the sixth."

"All ready?" queried Leslie.

"All ready," returned Kent.

Both bade Leland good-by, and after a few unimportant
words, started upon their journey. Leslie felt a wild, joyous
thrill as he realized that he was really nearing Rosalind; that

In a short time, as he firmly believed, he should see and be able to assist her to procure her liberty. He could hardly restrain his impatience, but vainly urged time to quicken his thoughtful, lagging steps. The sun had set, and darkness was slowly spreading over the great forest, when the two plunged into its depths and ventured upon their perilous, doubtful undertaking.

For a considerable time we have left Rosalind to herself, and with the reader's permission we will now return to her.

The Indians which held her, as was stated, journeyed far into the interior of Kentucky before making a final halt. Here they reached the village or head-quarters of their tribe; and gave her to understand that her journey was at an end.

The village numbered several hundred, and considering her defenseless position, the savages allowed her considerable liberty. From the first, however, she was made a slave and a drudge, and compelled to toil with the hardy squaws of their tribe, bearing their insults and sometimes even their blows. The hope and prospect of a speedy relief and deliverance enabled her to bear this without murmuring. She had not much fear of death, as she judged by their actions that their intention was to make her a prisoner for life.

There is nothing in the animal creation but which is affected by kindness and obedience, and there is no race upon which it makes a more ready impression than the American. Rosalind's continual gentleness and pleasing manner melted the hearts of many of the warriors, and more than one rude epithet was restrained by the meek loveliness of her face.

Yet she was sometimes in greater danger than she ever dreamed. All did not act and feel thus toward her; more than one voice demanded her blood, and while she lay quietly dreaming of some loved one, there was many an angry discussion over her life. Deadly, baleful glances were given her, when in her musings she was unconscious of the notice of any one; and among the entire female portion there was not a squaw but what regarded her with feelings of jealousy and hatred. Had she remained a month, at the end of that time her life would no doubt have been sacrificed. To quiet the continual broiling and angry feelings, the Indians would have acted as they did in nearly a similar case some years before;

she would have been tomahawked, as was the young Miss McCrea.

Rosalind often wondered who the person could be that had interrupted her conversation with Zeb upon the first night of her captivity. One day she was gratified with the knowledge. A savage approached her and commenced a conversation:

"How is the pale-faced maiden?"

She started at hearing her tongue spoken so well, and looking up recognized a middle-aged Indian, that had frequently visited her house during her father's life. She replied:

"Very well."

The savage was uneasy, and waited a few moments for her to speak further, but as she evinced no disposition to do so, he at length added:

"Does the maiden remember Pequanon?"

"She does," she returned, looking him steadily in the face. "She remembers him as one who received kindness both from her father's hand and her own, and as one who shows his gratitude by treacherously burning her home, and carrying her into captivity. Yes, Pequanon," she continued, bursting into tears at the remembrance of the event, "she remembers you and can never forget your conduct."

"Pequanon saved your life," he returned, feelingly.

"And gave me a fate that is worse."

"He went with his brothers when they burned your home, but he did not help. He went to save your life, and did do it. When the tomahawk was lifted over your head, he caught the arm and turned it aside. When your blood was called for, Pequanon swore that it should not be had, and he has kept his word. Pequanon never forgets kindness, and will die for the maiden that clothed and fed him."

Rosalind felt her heart moved with pity toward the poor, untutored savage who had thus really been grateful, and no doubt had done all in his power for her good. She recalled many instances where she believed that he was the cause of the lenity upon the part of the captors, and where it seemed that some one had shown an interest in her welfare. She informed him that she believed he had done her all the good that was in his power, and expressed her heartfelt thanks for it. The Indian seemed gratified beyond measure, and after further conversation took his departure, promising eternal fidelity to her.

This circumstance, though trivial in itself, had a great influence upon Rosalind. It gave her a knowledge of the true position in which she stood. Although she doubted not but that she had friends among the savage beings around her, yet she well knew that there were many deadly enemies, who, when an opportunity offered, would not hesitate to take her life. Every night when she lay down, it was with the prayer that her life might be preserved until morning, and that, were it in the power of her friends to rescue her, they would do it speedily.

The lodge in which she slept was that of the chief. Besides his own wife, several squaws remained in it during the night. A young woman, her most bitter and hateful enemy, slept beside Rosalind most of the time, and the slightest movement on the part of the latter was sure to occasion some insulting word or command from her. She bore this without a word, hoping each night that it was the last she was to spend in this manner.

One night she suddenly awoke to a full state of consciousness—so suddenly that it startled and alarmed her. It seemed as though something had awakened her, and yet she could recall nothing. She turned her head and gazed at her companion, but she, to all appearances, was sound asleep, and could not have been the cause. She experienced no more of
vsiness or inclination to sleep, but concluded to feign it
le hope of satisfying herself of any danger that might be
xing near her.
She half closed her eyes, yet kept a close watch of every
hing around her. In a moment there was a rustling upon
the outside; the next instant the point of a knife protruded through a gap in the skin of the lodge, and two eyes were seen gleaming like a tiger's; then the hand that held the knife was thrust forward, and it was held over her.

Rosalind tried to scream, but could not utter a sound. She seemed frozen with terror, and only made a spasmodic movement that awoke her companion. As soon as the latter moved, the hand was withdrawn and the rent closed of its own accord.

"Oh!" she murmured, "did you see it?"

Her companion, more angered on account of being awak-ened from her sleep, struck her a blow and commanded silence; but Rosalind could not remain in her position, and arising and stepping softly over the sleeping form beside her, seated herself in the center of the lodge. Here she remained until morning, when she made the inmates understand the nature of her nocturnal fright. All treated it lightly, and she began to entertain a suspicion that they knew more of it than she did herself.

In the course of the day she narrated the circumstance to Pequanon, showing him also the aperture that had been made in the lodge. He examined it carefully, and appeared trou-bled about it. The marks of a person's knee and moccasin could be seen upon the soft earth, and there was no doubt that her life had been sought. Pequanon informed her of something that surprised and alarmed her as much as this. Several of the warriors, since her first appearance among them, had shown a desire to obtain Rosalind for a wife; and although it may seem strange that she herself was not aware of the fact, Pequanon had noticed it from the commencement, and now for the first time warned her of it. One who sus-pected that he should be disappointed, had taken the means to procure the revenge that we have mentioned. Ever after this Pequanon remained in the lodge during the night, and Rosalind was careful to keep at a safe distance from the sides of it.

She saw in the fact that he had given her, the cause of the hatred upon the part of the females toward her. They had seen the favor with which she was regarded by numbers of the warriors, and were filled with jealousy at it. From them she had as much to fear as from the Indians who wished to obtain her.

CHAPTER XIV

THE RESCUE.

ROSALIND was a good distance from the Ohio, and consequently a long way was to be traveled by Kent and Leslie.
During the first night of their journey, a bright moon favored
them, and they continued on without halting until morning.
The hunter struck the trail at an early hour in the day, and
the two continued their pursuit with renewed ardor until the
sun was high in the heavens, when they halted for rest.

When they finally halted, it was on the banks of Big
Sandy, at the point where the West Fork unites with it.
Here they discovered signs of the encampment of a large
body of Indians. Leslie felt hope increase, and was impatient to pursue their way. They judged it best—or rather
Kent judged it best—to remain in their present position, and
follow the trail only during the day.

The hunter left Leslie in order to search for game, as they
both were exceedingly hungry. He returned in a short time,
to the surprise of Leslie, who had not heard the report of his
gun. Kent informed him that he had slain it without firing
a shot, as he dared not to risk one. A fire was started, it
being concealed by the river-bank as much as possible, and
their food was cooked. This finished, the fire was extinguished, and they partook of the repast.

A moon as bright as that of the preceding night arose,
and the clear river, glistening in the moonlight like liquid
silver, was visible for a great distance. Leslie was soon
asleep, but Kent lay awake the greater part of the night,
revolving in his mind the best course to pursue in regard to
capturing Rosalind. At last he hit upon the plan, and having fully determined what to do, he fell into a peaceful
slumber.

"Now to the rescue," said Leslie, springing to his feet as
soon as it was fairly light.

"I'd advise you to put a stopper on that jaw of yourn, if
you don't want the whole pack down here in a twinklin',"

quickly retorted the hunter, slowly coming to the sitting posture.

"Why, what's the matter, Kent?"

"Oh, nothin'; only there's a few Injins squatted over on t'other shore."

"Ah! well, they can't see us, at any rate, for a thick fog has gathered during the night and is resting upon the river."

"Wal, they can hear you easy 'nough, 'specially if you go on that way."

"Come, come, Kent, don't be cross. I'll wager that they haven't heard me, and I promise that they shall not."

The two shouldered their rifles, and, as the mist was slowly rising from the river, again commenced their journey. The trail was now easily discovered, and followed without difficulty. It led most of the time along the bank of the river, and its distinctness showed that the savages had no fear or cared little for pursuit. Instead of proceeding in Indian file, as they had at first, they traveled promiscuously and carelessly, and their number could be easily made out by their footsteps. During the course of the day Kent gave the exact number to Leslie, and the precise time that they had journeyed over the ground.

Leslie, in the ardor of his hopes, still had a fear that they might not really be upon the track of Rosalind. Might not some other party be misleading them? Was it not possible that the party had subdivided, and the one that held her taken an entirely different course? The probability of error prevented him from experiencing the joyous hopefulness that he might have otherwise felt. This worried and caused him so much anxiety, that he expressed his fears to Kent.

"Don't know but what we are," returned the hunter, composedly.

"Do you *think* that we are?" asked Leslie, earnestly.

"Can't say; I'll go back if you want to."

"Heigh! what's that?"

He sprung forward and caught a shred fluttering from a bush.

"That's it! that's it!" he shouted, fairly leaping with joy.

"That's what?" asked the hunter, seemingly disgusted at this display of childlike emotion.

"Why, a piece of her dress, sure enough," responded Leslie.

Here the corners of Kent's mouth gave a downward twitch, and turning his head so as to glance at Leslie, a deprecating grunt escaped him.

"She did it on purpose to guide us," added Leslie, not heeding him.

Kent's mouth jerked forward, and a loud guffaw was given.

"Let us hurry," said Leslie, starting forward.

"I allow," commenced the hunter, unable to restrain himself further, "that if you play many more such capers you'll go alone. If the sight of her dress sets you in such fits, what do you s'pose'll 'come of you when you set your eyes on her? and I daresn't think of the consequences of once gettin' your arm around her. Whew!"

"You must pardon my feeling, Kent; but the sudden assurance that we were not mistaken or proceeding by guess, completely overcame me."

"Somethin' queer come over you, no mistake."

"Well, if you don't like to see it, I will try and repress it in future."

"I hope you will when I'm about."

The two hurried on without further conversation for some time. At noon they made a shorter halt than usual, as Kent informed Leslie that, by pressing forward, they could gain the region of the savages by nightfall. As the afternoon advanced, the experienced eye of the hunter began to detect unmistakable signs of the presence of Indians.

Leslie could not repress his agitation as he realized that every minute was bringing him nearer and nearer to the object of his desires. Fear and hope filled him, and he was alternately gladdened by the one and tormented by the other.

He did not notice that Kent had changed his direction, and was proceeding more cautiously than before; he only knew that he was following closely in his footsteps, and relying entirely upon his guidance.

All at once the hunter came to a stop, and laid his hand upon Leslie's arm. He looked up, and there, before him, was the Indian village. Kent had conducted him to a sort of rising ground, which afforded them a complete view of it, while the forest gave them au effectual concealment.

"Is this the place?" asked he, in astonishment.

"This is the place," answered the ranger.

Leslie feasted his eyes a long time upon the scene before he withdrew his gaze. Every wigwam was visible, and the squaws and children could be seen passing to and fro through the sort of street or highway. Many of the warriors were gathered in groups, and reclined upon the ground, lazily chatting; while their far better halves were patiently toiling and drudging at the most difficult kinds of work.

Leslie scanned each form that came under his eye, in the hope of distinguishing *one;* but he was disappointed, and compelled to see the night closely settle over the village without obtaining a glimpse of her. "After all," he thought, "she may not be there, and I am doomed to be frustrated, at last." But again hope whispered in his ear, and rendered him impatient for the hour when his fate must be decided.

The moon arose at about midnight, consequently, all that was to be done must be done before that time. As soon as it had become fairly dark, so that Leslie was unable to distinguish any thing in the village, he seated himself beside Kent to ascertain his intentions.

"The time," said he, "has arrove when we must commence business, and I allow that we must be at it soon. Here's your part. You are to stay here till I come back. I am goin' down into their nest to hunt her up, and when I come back you'll know whether she's to be got or not. Keep quiet, and don't stir from this spot till I give you the order. Remember, if we're goin' to do any thin', you must do as I tell you. Take care of yourself."

With these words the hunter departed—departed so silently and stealthily, that Leslie hardly comprehended that he was gone.

Kent, while it was yet light, had taken a survey of the village, and viewed it, too, with a scout's eye. He had distinguished the chief's lodge from the others, and rightly conjectured that this would be the most likely to contain Rosalind. Accordingly, he determined to direct his footsteps toward it, before looking in any other direction. This was situated in the center. He was, consequently, exposed to greater danger in reaching it; yet he placed great reliance upon his disguise, which he yet assumed, and determined to venture within the village in a short time.

He stood at the extreme end, and now and then could discern a shadowy form passing silently before him, or, perhaps, the voice of some warrior or squaw; but soon these sights and sounds ceased, and he commenced moving forward. Not a savage was encountered until he stood before the lodge for which he was seeking. He had now reached the point where his most subtle powers of cunning were called into requisition, yet thought not of hesitating.

Standing a second in front of the lodge, he glanced about him, but not a form was to be seen. Had he been observed he must have been taken for an Indian, and attracted no further notice. Kent being certain that his way was clear, sunk to the earth, and lying upon his face, worked himself slowly and cautiously toward the lodge. He seemed to glide precisely like a serpent, so easy and silent were his motions. In a moment he was beside it, and, as he believed, within ten feet of the object of his search. A dim light was burning. By its light he hoped to satisfy himself shortly of the truth of his conjectures. Running the keen point of his knife along the skin that formed the lodge, he had pierced it enough to admit his gaze, when the light was suddenly extinguished.

For a moment the hunter's calculations were at fault. He had not counted upon this, but had hoped to gain a view of the interior while the light was burning. He felt barely able to repress his disappointment, as he was again compelled to devise some other plan. For once he had been frustrated in his design, and he felt it keenly.

But he determined to risk a look at all hazards. The aperture was completed; Kent raised his head and peered in—and betrayed himself.

Pequanon was at his place in the inside as usual, watching.

In the nobleness of his soul, the life of Rosalind. His quick ear detected the noise, slight as it was, occasioned by Kent's labor. The latter supposing the inmates of the lodge would be slumbering, hoped for an opportunity to do what he wished. But Pequanon was on the alert, and detected him at work. When his face was placed at the opening, it was brought between the sky and the darkness of the lodge, and the Indian plainly observed the outlines of his face. His first impulse was to seize a rifle and shoot the intruder instantly, for he believed that it was the one who sought the life of Rosalind; but checking himself, he arose and passed out noiselessly, determined to satisfy himself before action.

Two consummate hunters were now maneuvering against each other. The movements of both with respect to themselves were as much at fault as though they were inexperienced youngsters. The noise of Pequanon was so slight that it failed to awake either Rosalind or any of the inmates; yet Kent heard it distinctly, and crouched down upon the ground and listened. In an instant he caught the step upon the outside. He knew that he could spring to his feet and easily make his escape; but in doing so, he would raise an alarm, and thus effectually prevent any thing of use being done by himself. He therefore withdrew some ten or fifteen feet, and trusted that the Indian would not search further; but he was mistaken. Pequanon was determined to satisfy himself in regard to Rosalind's secret enemy; and espying the shadowy form gliding along from him, he sprung toward it, hoping and expecting that it might leap to its feet.

The form leaped to its feet in a manner that he little suspected. Kent saw that an encounter was unavoidable, when, concentrating his strength, he bounded like a panther toward the savage, bearing him to the earth, with his iron hand clutching his throat. Pequanon struggled, but was powerless, and could not make a sound above a painful gurgle. Kent whipped out his knife, and had just aimed at his breast, when the savage found voice to speak a few words.

"Hold! you strike the white man's friend!"

The excellent English startled Kent, and he relaxed his hold.

"Who are you?" he demanded.

"Pequanon, the white man's friend."

"What did you come nosin' out here fur then?"

Kent's knees were upon the arms of the Indian, while he was seated upon his breast. The hunter loosed his grasp.

"The pale-faced maiden. Pequanon wished to save her."

"Wal, see here, old redskin, I'm after her. You's sayin' as how you's her friend. Mind to help?"

The Indian answered in the affirmative.

"Wal, I'll let you up, pervidin' you'll go and bring her out What you say?"

"Is it her friends that wish her?"

"You've hit it there. Goin' to help?"

"Pequanon will lay his life down for the captive."

"I'll let you up then, and give you two minutes to trot her out. If you undertake to come any of your tricks over me, I'll blow your brains out."

Kent permitted Pequanon to arise, who departed silently for the lodge without giving a reply to his remark.

The hunter was not to be deceived by any artifice of the savage, and to guard against treachery, withdrew still further from the lodge. He doubted very much whether the Indian would endeavor to assist him at all, but he had done the best he could under the circumstances.

In a moment his doubts were put to flight by the re-appearance of the noble Indian, with Rosalind. As cool and collected as was the hunter, he could not repress a joyous start as he gazed upon her form.

"That's the fust Injin, accordin' to my opinc," he muttered to himself, "that ever *was* a man."

Rosalind, all trembling eagerness and anxiety, on coming up to Kent, seemed unable to speak. The hunter noticed her action and forebore speaking, making a motion, as an apology, for silence. For a second the trio remained motionless and undetermined what course to pursue. Pequanon noticed this and started toward the river.

"Hold on, cap'n!" said Kent; "there's another chap that come with me."

The hunter now took the lead; and leaving them hopefully pursuing their way, let us glance at Leslie until they arrive.

Chafing, fretting, hoping, fearing and doubting sat Leslie, impatiently awaiting the appearance of Kent. The falling of a leaf, or rustling of the branches under some light breeze startled him ; and when a night-bird, that had been resting above him gave utterance to its unearthly hoot, and swooped past, its voice he mistook for the yell of his savage foes, and the flap of its wings for their approaching tread.

Now he pictured the bliss that he hoped to feel ; then again he was the prey of most poignant doubts and fears. Would he see her, and clasp her to his bosom, or was she a hopeless captive ? Was she living or dead ? Would Kent come back without information or hope ? Suddenly there arose a wild, prolonged yell, that fairly froze him with terror. Kent was discovered, and all hope was gone ! Oh, the agony of that moment !

Hardly comprehending the state of things, he formed a dozen different plans at once. Now he was going to rush madly forward and rescue Rosalind during the confusion, and then was about shouting for Kent.

All at once he heard a footstep. The pursuers were then at hand ! Resolved to lay one savage low, he rushed forward toward the approaching figure. Could it be possible ? Was it not a dream ? There she stood before his eyes. His limbs trembled, and he felt upon the point of falling.

"Is this Mr. Leslie ?" asked a sweet voice that had thrilled him more than once before.

"I guess it's him or his spook," answered Kent, for him. "If there's goin' to be any huggin' done, hurry up with it, fur they're follerin' us."

This threw off all reserve. Leslie folded Rosalind to his breast. She spoke not—resisted not—her trembling limbs and sobs told more than words could have done.

"That'll do for the present," interrupted Kent, in a kind tone. "We must be off now, fur the red-skins have smelt the rat, and I should judge by the noise they're makin' that they're in a confounded muss. Never mind, don't cry. When we get down home out of danger I'll let you hug and cry as much as you please. Which way, Mr. Redskin ?"

Pequauon turned to the left and took long, impatient strides. Kent followed closely in his footsteps, while

Leslie led the trembling Rosalind. Often, regardless of tho danger which threatened, he pressed her to him and whispered words of which we can only guess the meaning.

On they hurried, half running, over the tangled underwood and fallen trees until they paused upon the brink of the river.

Here, to the surprise and joy of all, Pequanon running to a clump of bushes pulled forth a large canoe and shoved it into the stream. The others needed no admonition to use it.

"Here," said their guide, "we part. May the Great Spirit guide you."

"Say, you, you'll get into trouble, won't you, if you go back?" queried Kent.

"The Great Spirit will protect me. Farewell."

"Wait, Pequanon," said Rosalind, rising from her seat.

"Pequanon has only paid his debt to the pale-faced maiden." The Indian was gone.

Rosalind sunk back upon her seat in tears.

"He's the first Injin that I ever got my clutches on that has got away after it, and the first one that I ever felt like lettin' go. Somehow or other my old gun didn't burn and wriggle when I sot my eyes on him, as it is used to doin' in such cases; and if it wasn't fur that red hide of hisn, I wouldn't believe he was one of them."

All this time the shouts and yells of the savages could be heard, and now and then it seemed to the fugitives that they must have been discovered. Kent pulled the boat to the opposite shore, and as he expressed it, "hugged the bank mighty close." He had little fear of being discovered, but the utmost caution was to be used, for, in their rage, the savages would use every means in their power to recapture them.

Kent knew that by keeping on, he would in time reach the banks of the Ohio. Their enemies would probably suspect the true nature of their escape and take to the river in pursuit; and, as the Indians, in case of discovery, could easily overtake and recapture them, they must necessarily be saved by fortune and stratagem. Though scarce a ripple was heard, the shadowy form of the boat shot swiftly under the hanging trees and round the projecting points of the bank, like some serpent gliding noiselessly over the surface.

Soon the edge of the great moon slowly rose above the

dark line of the forest, and its long rays streamed over wood
and river; when it had finally risen high up in the heavens,
the stream shone as brightly as at noonday. Its winding
course could be discerned ahead until it was lost in the forest,
and for miles behind, its banks were as clearly defined as it
could have been under the sun's rays.

Now that the river and its objects were so plainly de-
picted, Kent kept closer yet under the shadows of the friendly
bank. Now and then he hurried through some opening in
the trees of the shore, where, for a minute, he was exposed
to any gaze that might chance to be given; then, when the
water was shallow, he struck the muddy bottom, and
patiently worked himself on again. Being engaged in rowing, his face was turned toward the stern, and thus had a ful
sweep of the river which he had passed over, the only point
from which he had reason to apprehend danger.

He was upon the point of speaking, when his quick eye
detected a speck in view around a bend in the river, some
distance back. He halted, for he knew its character.

"We're follered!" said he, guiding the boat in to shore.

A few minutes more and the boat could be plainly seen by
all three. It was in the center of the stream, and approaching rapidly. The heads of four or five Indians could be discerned. Their object was plain to all.

Kent had run his boat against the shore, and the three
were now waiting breathlessly for their enemies to pass.

The Indians plainly had no suspicion that the fugitives
were so close at hand, and kept steadily onward. Hardly
daring to breathe, our three friends saw the long, sharp canoe,
with five of their mortal enemies, shoot past, and disappear.

"Did you see how my gun kept twitchin' and jumpin'?
Why, I had all I could do to hold him. Thunder! it's too
bad to see them fellers give you such a nice shot and then
miss it," said the ranger, again taking the oars.

Kent now guided the boat with greater caution, ever and
anon turning and looking ahead, not daring to leave the sole
watch to Leslie, who had other things far more interesting to
himself with which to occupy his mind.

CHAPTER XV

THE FUGITIVES FLYING NO LONGER.

THE fugitives continued moving forward until morning, when, to guard against needless exposure, Kent again ran the canoe under the bank, and remained at rest the entire day. All suffered so much from hunger, that the hunter left the boat during the afternoon, and, after a few hours' absence, obtained a sufficient quantity of meat for them all. This was cooked after his usual cautious and expert fashion, and was thankfully partaken of by his companions.

Roland and the maid were resting on the sheltered bank of the river; none but Kent ventured out of sight of the spot during the day. For aught they knew there might be hordes of savages within hearing of their voices, scouring the woods in every direction in their search; it needed but the slightest inadvertency upon their part to insure their own destruction.

Leslie sat conversing with Rosalind, when Kent started up, and, glancing behind, stepped down the river-bank and peered out upon the stream. Leslie was beside him in an instant, and, as the two gazed out, the boat which they had seen pursuing them during the night came into view. It was coming up-stream, evidently returning from the chase. It now contained but three savages. Although Leslie had but little to fear, nevertheless he watched the boat with intense interest. Pausing a second, he glanced around, and exclaimed, in terror:

"As sure as heaven, they are heading toward this point."

Kent commanded, in a whisper:

"Get your shootin'-iron ready, and be ready yourself "They're comin' in below us'"

The savages had landed a few hundred yards down-stream, and seemed to suspect the presence of no one. Suddenly one of them uttered a loud whoop. In a moment it was repeated, and an answer came, apparently from a distance. Ere long two savages approached the canoe. and, entering, the five again shoved out, and commenced paddling up-stream. Leslie asked Kent the meaning of these proceedings.

"Plain enough," he answered; "they left them two fellers on the shore last night, so that, if they passed us, they would see us when we came along, and they've been watching there ever since. If we'd gone a half a mile further, they'd have shot us; but as we happeued to stop afore they got eyes on us, they've missed us, that's all."

At night they again set out, proceeding fearlessly. When morning again dawned, many miles were placed between Rosalind and her captors.

It is needless to dwell upon the further particulars of their homeward journey. Every day occupied was like its predecessor: pressing boldly forward when the shade of night favored them; proceeding more cautiously through the day; resting sometimes in the center of the stream, and then again approaching the shore for food; uow a prey to some imaginary fear, and then thrilling with hope, when they finally glided into the fair Ohio. Safely they reached their destination unpursued, and fearing uo enemy.

"Wouder who's iu them pile of logs up thar," remarked Kent, glancing suspiciously at Leslie, when they were approaching the ruius of the house.

"Why, who would be there?" returned he, with well-feigned ignorance.

"Looks as though somebody had fitted it up. Hallo, here!" demanded Kent, battering against the structure.

At this summons George Leland stepped forth.

The meeting was such as can be easily imagined; joy complete filled the hearts of all; friend, brother, sister and lover were reunited; nothing was wanting to fill their cup of bliss. The old hunter, as soon as his brief salutation was over, withdrew to the background. Leaning on his rifle, he remarked that he was "goin' to look on and see the fun."

As soon as the emotiou of all had subsided, they turned toward the hunter. They were without shelter and home, aud something must be done at oucc.

Kent at once divined their thoughts and said: "Wal, sit down and I'll tell you what's to be doue."

The three did as required, and Kent unfolded his plan.

" There's too much trouble for you in these parts; you must•leave. Up the river some distance is quite a settlement, and there's the only place you can stay. What I propose is this: we must leave here as soon as possible, and let us do it *now.*"

" More than once have I thought of the plan which Kent has given," said Leslie, "and I hope that it will be carried out at the earliest moment. Every hour passed here is an hour of peril.

" The matter is then settled," said George. " Let us prepare to pass our last night here; then to seek another home."

The shelter in which Leland had spent his time during the absence of the others was found to be commodious enough to accommodate all, and into it they went. The old hunter kept watch during the night, while the rest slept, and we doubt very much whether four happier, more hopeful beings ever were congregated.

At the earliest streak of morn, the hunter aroused the others, and they prepared to take their final departure. The canoe in which the three had come was found to be sufficiently capacious for the entire party. With a tear of regret for the old home, the fair Rosalind entered the canoe, and soon it was cutting the waters on its upward course.

It is not necessary in this place to dwell upon the particulars of their journey. They encountered nothing unusual or alarming until, in rounding a bend in the river, they were startled by the sight of an unusual object far up the stream. With the exception of Kent, all manifested considerable surprise and apprehension.

" What are we to encounter now?" asked Leslie, as he earnestly scrutinized the approaching object. " Are we never to be rid of these brutes?"

" It is undoubtedly one of their contrivances," added Leland, "and I'm afraid we shall have to take to the woods again to give it a go-by. How is it, Kent?"

The face of the hunter wore a quizzical look, and his only reply was a quiet smile. As he observed the looks of wonder his companions cast upon him, he became more thoughtful.

" This is bad business," said he, shaking his head; " *that* is something I didn't expect to see."

The progress of the canoe by this time was checked, and it was drifting with the current. The two young men had no desire for a nearer approach to the apparently formidable contrivance.

"Can't either one of you two chaps make out what sort of ship that is coming down-stream?"

Both Leland and Leslie were considerably puzzled, when they saw Rosalind smile, as if enjoying their stupidity.

"If you can't tell, just ask the gal," added the hunter, bursting into a loud laugh.

"Why, George, I thought you had lived long enough in the western country to recognize a *flat-boat!*"

"What dunces we both were. How could any one imagine that to be any thing else than a genuine flat-boat? Let us approach it and make the acquaintance of those on board."

"Sart'in boys," said the hunter, dipping his paddles deep into the water and impelling the canoe rapidly forward.

"A cheer for them!" exclaimed Leslie, rising in the boat and swinging his hat over his head.

How unspeakably thankful were the hearts of the fugitives, as their salutation was returned by more than one voice Friends indeed were near, and their dangers were over.

A few moments later the canoe was beside the flat-boat.

"Thank God! thank God!" fervently uttered Leland, as he clasped his sister in his arms and realized that they were now safe, safe! For the first time in weeks he felt the sweet consciousness of safety.

"It is almost worth the sufferings we have undergone!" said he. "This sweet consciousness that we are really beyond the reach of our foes is an enjoyment that we have not experienced for a long time."

"Do not forget the all-sustaining Hand that has brought us out of the very jaws of death."

"Forget it? May He forget me when I fail to remember Him. Great Father," said Leland, meekly uncovering and bowing his head, while the tears fell like rain down his face, "Great Father, for this and all other mercies I thank thee!"

"I join my thanksgiving with theirs," said Leslie, in the same reverent manner, as he approached brother and sister.

The flat-boat was no other than the celebrated expedition

under Major Taylor, which established such a firm and pros-
perous settlement upon the northern bank of the Ohio. He
had about thirty souls on board, a dozen of whom were men.
The true cause of the astonishing success of this company was
that both the leader and his comrades fully understood the
perils they encountered in venturing into the great western
wilderness. They were not men who could be decoyed into
the simplest or most cunning contrivances that Indian inge-
nuity could suggest, nor were they those who expected to
spend a life of ease and enjoyment in the woods. They
simply understood and prepared for what was before them.

Major Taylor was a man rather inclined to corpulency, with
a red face, Roman nose and eagle eye that seemed to pene-
trate every thing at which it glanced. He was very affable
and social, a great favorite among all his acquaintances,
especially the female portion, who always felt safe in his presence. His men, nearly all of whom had served under him in
the Revolution, trusted implicitly in him.

"Friends, you are welcome, doubly welcome to this boat,"
said he, raising his hat and saluting Rosalind with all the
stately politeness of a gentleman of the old school. "I trust
your stay upon it will be as prolonged as our own, who, in
all probability, will be the last passengers it will ever carry."

Leslie related in a few words the main facts concerning the
burning of Leland's home, the capture and subsequent escape
of himself and sister, and finally of their desire to reach the
upper settlements. The commiserations of all were given
them. For Rosalind especially they seemed unable to do
enough. She was taken within their cabin, where every
thing that was possible was done for her comfort.

"I must now insist that you remain with us," said Major
Taylor. "Now that you have no home to which to return,
you must accompany us and build a new one. If the red-
skins take *our* homes from us they are welcome to do so ; but
when they undertake it, I suspect they will find they are
troubling a set of men that know a trick or two as well as
themselves. We've all seen service among the dogs."

"Do you think, Cap'n, there's likely to be a scrimmage
where you drive your stakes ?" inquired Kent, with a considerable degree of curiosity.

"I am sure I can not tell," replied Major Taylor. "It cer tainly seems probable, but why do you ask?"

" 'Cause if there's any likelibility of it, I'll agree to accep. your invite and go with you."

"Well, well, my good man, you will go with us any way, and take the chances of a brush with them. You strike me as a man who has seen considerable of the woods."

" He has indeed," said Leslie. " Under heaven, our safety is owing to his experience and sagacity. He has spent a lifetime in the woods, and I can honestly say he will be a valuable acquisition to your party."

" Come, none of that now, or I'll leave you!" said the hunter, in a warning tone to his young friend.

"I have no doubt of it—no doubt of it in the least. We need him, and if he will only go with us, I think I can promise that he will occasionally see the service for which his soul longs. But, you have not given us your decision."

" We are very grateful for your offer," said Leland ; " we have indeed no other refuge to which we can go. The house which has sheltered my sister and myself since infancy is swept away by those whom we had learned to look upon as our friends and protectors. I think when we see men at your age beginning life again, we can afford to do it ourselves."

" Of course you can—of course you can," replied the officer, in his hearty manner. " We'll start a settlement on a grand scale. One of our men once took orders, and is licensed to marry, so that if either of you gentlemen should need his services at *any* time, you will always find him at hand."

" There is a servant—a negro, who was taken at the same time with my sister. I feel as though some effort should be made to recover him," added Leland, a few minutes later. "We shall be in a situation to do that by accompanying you, or, at least, we shall be more likely to find some means of doing so, than if we followed out the idea, entertained some time ago, of leaving the country altogether."

" I am decidedly of the opinion—"

The officer was interrupted by a man at the front of the boat, calling out his name. He instantly hastened beside him, and demanded what he wanted.

" Yonder is something approaching, and I can not satisfy

myself as to what it is. What do you make of it?" he asked.

Major Taylor bent his sharp gaze upon the object in question for a moment, and then replied:

"It looks like the head of a person, and yet it is certainly an odd-looking head. We will call this hunter that has just come on board. Undoubtedly he can assist us."

In answer to the summons, Kent approached the bow of the boat, rifle in hand. He peered across the water, but for a time, failed to identify the thing.

"Stand back a little, and I'll give it a shot. I'll graze it at first, so as to be sure of what I am going to hit when L shoot next time."

The hunter raised his rifle, and holding it a second, fired. At the same instant the unknown object disappeared.

"I think you struck it!" remarked Leland.

"I didn't aim *at* it, and consequently it ain't been hit,' returned Kent, with an air of assurance.

"Yonder it is this moment!"

As these words were uttered, it again appeared, and to the amazement of all, called out to them:

"Gorra! what you wastin' your bullets on dis nigger's head for? Reckoned Kent knowed better."

The hunter seemed on the point of falling from laughter.

"Who'd a thought it was Zeb! Where has he come from? He beats all niggers in Kentuck for adventures and walloping lies."

A few minutes later the negro was received upon the flatboat. It is scarcely necessary to say that his friends all experienced unfeigned joy at his return. He was as jubilant and reckless of the truth as ever, and it was a long time before they got at the truth regarding his escape from the Shawnees.

The flight of Leland, under Providence, was really the means of liberating the negro. The confusion occasioned by the escape of the former was so great, that the savages imagined he also had fled with him. Understanding that it was "do or die" with him, he tugged and struggled at his bonds with the strength of desperation. Being secured to a tree as usual, at some distance from the center of confusion, he escaped observation for a few moments. It is doubtful, however, whether he would have succeeded in freeing himself, had he not been covertly assisted by some unknown friend. Who this personage could be, was never known ; perhaps some Indian who had been befriended by the Leland family, and who experienced some compunctions of honor (not of conscience) at the situation of the poor negro.

Zeb had learned enough by this time to exercise a little common sense. Accordingly, when he found himself free, he made the best use of his feet and wits, and used every effort to reach the Ohio river. According to his own narration, he overcame all manner of perils before succeeding. Undoubtedly he incurred great risk in the undertaking, and finally succeeded.

He was trudging wearily along the river margin, listening for some sound of his relentless enemies, who, he doubted not, were upon his trail, when he caught sight of the flat-boat. Although he did not identify it at once, he understood from its size and formation that the hand of the white man alone was concerned in its structure. He immediately plunged into the river, reaching it in due time, as we have already shown.

At last the pioneers reached their destination, and began a settlement which, at this day, is not a town merely but a flourishing city. As we have hinted in another place, their experience of frontier life and the sagacity and foresight of their nominal head, saved them from the misfortunes and sufferings that often befall settlers in the new country. It is true the red wave of the dreadful war in the West surged to their very doors ; but they saw far away in the heavens the portentous signs, and so prepared that they passed through it unscathed.

The passing years touched lightly the heads of Roland and Rosalind Leslie. As the palmy days of peace settled upon them, an old hunter frequently spent days and weeks at their house. At such times, he took the children upon his knees, and told them of the hardships and suffering their parents had endured, and recounted many of his own adventures to them. Old Kent was a universal favorite in the settlement. As he became too old to spend his time entirely in the woods,

he joined the boys in their hunts, and there was not one who
would not have braved death in his defense.   He died peace-
fully and happily, under the roof of those whom he had served
so well, and was given a burial, at his own request, in the
grand old woods which had ever been his delight and enjoyment.

The wife of Leland survived all of those who have fig-
ured in these pages; but she too has been laid in the
valley.   Their descendants are now a numerous and influen-
tial family, proud of their ancestry, and enthusiastic over the
deeds of THE RANGER.

THE END.